SHARPEN YOUR TEAM'S SKILLS IN
*C*OACHING

Other titles in this series

Sharpen your skills in motivating people to perform
Trevor Bentley 007 709072 1

Sharpen your team's skills in effective selling
Trevor Bentley   007 709279 1

Sharpen your team's skills in developing strategy
Susan Clayton   007 709281 3

Sharpen your team's skills in creativity
Trevor Bentley   007 709282 1

Sharpen your team's skills in project management
Jean Harris   007 709140 X

Sharpen your team's skills in supervision
Susan Clayton   007 709280 5

Sharpen your team's skills in people skills
Di Kamp   007 709276 7

Sharpen your team's skills in time management
Jane Allan   007 709275 9

SHARPEN YOUR TEAM'S SKILLS IN

COACHING

Tony Voss

The McGraw-Hill Companies

London · New York · St Louis · San Francisco · Auckland · Bogotá · Caracas
Lisbon · Madrid · Mexico · Milan · Montreal · New Delhi · Panama · Paris
San Juan · São Paulo · Singapore · Sydney · Tokyo · Toronto

Published by
McGraw-Hill Publishing Company
Shoppenhangers Road, Maidenhead, Berkshire, SL6 2QL, England
Telephone 01628 502500
Facsimile 01628 770224

British Library Cataloguing in Publication Data
Voss, Tony
  Sharpen your team's skills in coaching
  1. Employees – Training of 2. Employee training personnel
  I. Title II. Coaching
  658.3′12404

  ISBN 0-07-709278-3

Library of Congress Cataloging-in-Publication Data
Voss, Tony
    Sharpen your team's skills in coaching / Tony Voss.
      p. cm.
    "Based on an original work by Dennis Kinlaw, The ASTD trainer's
  sourcebook: coaching ... McGraw-Hill, New York 1996"—T.p. verso.
    Includes bibliographical references and index.
    ISBN 0-07-709278-3 (pbk. : alk. paper)
    1. Work groups—Management. 2. Managers—Training of.
  3. Employees—Training of. 4. Employee motivation. I. Kinlaw,
  Dennis C Coaching. II. Title. III. Title: Coaching.
  HD66.V675 1996
  658.4′036–DC20   96-36299
                                                                  CIP

Based on an original work by Dennis Kinlaw, *The ASTD Trainer's
Sourcebook: Coaching* (0 07 053443 8) McGraw-Hill, New York, 1996

McGraw-Hill

A Division of The McGraw·Hill Companies

12345 CUP 9987

Typeset by BookEns Ltd, Royston, Herts
Printed and bound in Great Britain at the University Press, Cambridge

Printed on permanent paper in compliance with ISO Standard 9706

CONTENTS

EXERCISES

SERIES PREFACE

This series of books focuses on sharpening the performance of your team by providing a range of training and support materials. These materials can be used in a variety of ways to improve the knowledge and skills of your team.

The creation of high performance is achieved by paying attention to three key elements:

- The skills or competencies of your people
- The way these skills are applied
- The support your people receive from you in applying their skills.

SKILL DEVELOPMENT

The books in this series will provide materials for the development of a range of skills on a subject-by-subject basis. Each book will provide information and exercises in manageable chunks (lessons), which will be presented in a format that will allow you to choose the most appropriate way to deliver them to your staff. The contents will consist of all you need to guide your staff to a full understanding of the subject.

There are at least four ways you could choose to guide the learning of your team, these are:

- Training sessions
- Learning groups
- Open learning
- Experiential learning.

TRAINING SESSIONS

These can be run by bringing your people together and guiding them step by step through the materials, including the exercises. During these sessions you can invite your people to interact with you and the materials by asking questions and relating the materials to their current work. The materials will provide you with the detailed information you need to present the subject to your team.

LEARNING GROUPS

This approach involves dividing your team into small groups (two, three or four people) and having a brief session with each group, introducing them to the materials. Each group then works through the materials and meets with you from time to time to assess progress and receive your guidance.

OPEN LEARNING

This approach invites your people to use the materials at their own speed and in their own way. This is a form of individual learning that can be managed by regular meetings between you and your team as individuals or in a group. The process is started by introducing the materials to your team and agreeing some 'learning outcomes' to be achieved.

EXPERIENTIAL LEARNING

This calls for you to invite your team to examine the materials using the exercises as a focus, and then to get them to relate what they are learning directly to real-life situations in the workplace. This experience of learning is then shared and discussed by the team as a whole.

The books in the series have been designed to enable these four approaches to be used, as well as other ways that you might think are more appropriate to your team's specific needs.

APPLYING SKILLS

Time spent developing skills can be wasted if people do not have the opportunity to practise them. It is important that you consider this aspect of performance before embarking on a particular programme. It is useful to be able clearly to identify opportunities for practising skills and to discuss these with your team. Providing opportunities for practising and further developing competency is part and parcel of the whole approach of this series.

PROVIDING SUPPORT

Once people have acquired a new skill and have been provided with opportunities to apply it, they still need your support and coaching while they are experimenting with using it. The opening book in this series, *Sharpen your skills in motivating people to perform*, provides clear guidance on how to help people to develop their skills and then how to provide experience, practice and support as they use these skills.

Before starting work with your team on the materials in this book I suggest you do the following:

1. Review the materials yourself
2. Plan the approach you are going to follow
3. Discuss with your team what you are planning
4. Agree some learning outcomes
5. Indicate how you are going to support your team during the learning process.

You can also make the materials relate to your specific circumstances by doing three things:

- Add local 'colour'
- Adjust the emphasis
- Integrate your own materials.

The authors in the series have endeavoured to provide a range of materials that is comprehensive and will support you and your team. I hope that during this process you learn from and enjoy the experience.

Dr Trevor J. Bentley
Series Editor

ABOUT THE EDITORIAL PANEL

Dr Trevor Bentley, series editor for this series, is a freelance organizational consultant, a facilitator and a writer. Prior to becoming a consultant and while working as a senior executive, Trevor carried out a major research project into decision making and organization structures for which he was awarded his PhD. Over the last 20 years he has had a wide range of experience working with organizations in over 20 countries. Trevor has trained for four years with Gestalt South West and has attended Gestalt workshops in the UK and Europe. He now applies a Gestalt approach in his work.

Trevor has written 20 books and over 250 articles on business-related issues. His background includes careers as a management accountant, financial director, computer systems designer, a management services manager, a human–computer interface consultant, a trainer and a business manager. His current area of interest is in the application of a Gestalt approach to solving problems of organizational harmony. This includes culture change, performance management, team facilitation, executive coaching, mentoring and integrated supervision.

Susan Clayton is a leading contributor to the use and development of Gestalt philosophy and practice in organizations. Focusing on human processes, she enables managers and their staff to achieve business goals that depend on managing people. Her skill in raising awareness of how people relate to each other can forge supportive alliances and powerful co-operative relationships. Her approach includes helping people to manage blocks and difficulties in their contact with others, clearing the way for work and business relationships to move forward and grow.

Susan works with managers at all levels. Her interventions have aided groups in turmoil, managers needing to reach common agreement and individuals needing mentoring and coaching support. She helps organizations understand how to manage in a way that creates trust, respect and clarity in human relationships.

Mike Taylor is a consultant involved in the design, implementation and facilitation of personal and team development programmes within organizations. Since graduating in 1987, he has worked with two outdoor management training providers, both as a manager and tutor. His work has a strong focus on the use of experiential learning in developing managers, mainly within larger organizations.

Mike also works with groups and single individuals in running meetings and events that help teams and individuals explore working practices and approaches. More recently he has developed an interest in Gestalt as a way of understanding group processes. He is a member of the Association for Management Education and Development.

ABOUT THE AUTHOR

Dr **Tony Voss** is a counsellor, consultant and trainer. He originally trained as a chemist before working in environmental research developing sea-going computer systems and information technology, and later in the computer industry as a project manager, consultant and quality manager. Tony has a particular interest in enabling people to contribute fully and creatively to their endeavours, and sees this as benefiting individuals, their organizations and society at large. He is an Accredited Counsellor with the British Association for Counselling, and he has also trained in Gestalt over four years.

Tony works with those wanting to develop their organization and people, and those dealing with particular challenges in their working life. His clients also include those exploring the role of work in their life, as well as those with more personal issues. He can be contacted by e-mail at: tv@antipole.demon.co.uk

ACKNOWLEDGEMENTS

The questionnaire on leadership style in Exercise 1 is used with permission of McGraw-Hill.

My thanks are due to Sue Mbuiya Clayton for permission to reproduce her calligraphy in Figure 8.1 (page 83).

CHAPTER 1

INTRODUCTION

> **The only way in which anyone can lead us is to restore to us the belief in our own guidance.**
>
> (Henry Miller 1941)

PURPOSE OF THIS BOOK

This is a book for people who want to develop the coaching approach within their organization. In the spirit of coaching, it presents an opportunity for managers and their people to learn this approach together. The focus is not just on how to adopt the coaching approach yourself (although you can use it this way), but on how to help your people become coaches themselves. Not only will the 'manager' learn to coach his or her people, but these people will simultaneously learn to become coaches to their people or those for whom they will later be responsible.

The focus in this book is on learning together.

Traditionally, a manager may teach his people a skill that he himself already has. Alternatively he may read up on a subject and then present his knowledge to his people. Although you could work in that way, my invitation to you is not to keep this book to yourself but to share it with your people so that you can all learn from it together. The book thus becomes a resource that you can use with your people and that they in turn can use with their people. In this way you will be passing on the skills. The difference may seem small, but it is the start of breaking with the idea that the manager should know the subject first or better. This is an important step in moving towards a process of learning together.

This book, and indeed the whole series of books, recognizes that many managers are busy people who do not have time to set aside for a training course, and who may also not be able to spare their people for training. In any event, when training is provided outside the work setting, it can be difficult to integrate the learning and apply it in practice.

I have written this book so that coaching skills can be developed within the work setting and with minimal disruption to commitments. As the new skills are developed *in situ*, their application is a natural process.

WHY COACHING?

THE CHALLENGE FOR MANAGERS

Traditionally, managers were people who knew how the work in their department should be done. Because they did not have time to do it all themselves, they engaged others to help them and directed them by telling them what had to be done and how to do it. These other people were the manager's servants, whose role was to support the manager in the achievement of his objectives.

Over the past 10 or 15 years, progressive organizations have faced the limitations of this model. The rapid pace of change means that managers cannot expect to know everything about what goes on in their departments. The ever increasing expectation to achieve more in less time can leave managers burdened by responsibility. Managers need to move beyond being skilled in the tasks allocated to their particular departments, to being skilled in managing the people and teams who perform these tasks.

Traditional management practice is limiting.

Progressive organizations have seen the frustration of people limited by their role in serving the needs of their managers. They have realized that modern education prepares younger people not for servantship but for inquiry, discovery and initiative. The best of them tire quickly if they do not have scope to use their talents in this way, and they move on to new opportunities. Organizations that cling to the traditional model end up as frustrating and limiting places with low energy and limited achievement.

If we are to engage today's up-and-coming generation of people and to benefit from their talents, we need to rethink the role of managers and the task of leadership. Common to this new thinking is the process of turning the issue upside down: in other words, fostering the idea that the leader's function is to support and encourage his or her people in carrying out the tasks of the organization rather than to direct and control them. Management theorists now talk about 'servant leadership' and organizations are moving away from traditional titles such as *manager* towards *team leader, lead associate* or *coaching supervisor*.

We need to turn management practice upside down.

This change is not an easy one for those steeped in traditional approaches. We all learn primarily from example. Those of us who grew up through traditional management hierarchies may feel most comfortable when we organize our people in the way we were once organized. Our people, too, may have learnt to expect this organization and to value its predictability. They may feel unsettled or insecure when change is in the air.

New thinking requires us to change too.

The challenge for us is to let go of old and tired approaches. We need to support our people in developing their skills and abilities in the task of the organization, as new generation leaders, and as fulfilled and creative people.

THE SPORTS COACH

The role of the coach is well established in the sports field. All the great teams or sports people have behind them a coach who helps them achieve their goals and ambitions, even though this individual may not be known to the public. Torvill and Dean, the ice-dance champions, are virtually household names who drew a huge following at the peak of their careers. Their coach Betty Callaway was a vital

The sports coach is a model for the idea of management coaching.

instrument in their development. Few of their public know of her, although she is certainly well known within the ice skating world and recognized for her coaching skills. While Betty had a background as a skater herself, she never skated in competitions. It is said that she is an outstanding trainer because she has to work things out the hard way for herself, and thus knows how to help others learn (Hennessy, 1983). It is difficult to learn from those who do everything effortlessly or as if by magic. A good coach is able to show simply how things are done and how they can be learned.

The sports coach gives us some important insights into the role of coaches.

1. The coach's task is to help the pupil achieve excellence.
2. The focus is on the pupil, and not the coach.
3. Superior coaches are the ones whose pupils achieve continuous improvements in performance.
4. The coach may have skill in the activity but does not expect to match the pupil's skills. Indeed the coach's contribution is to support the pupil in achieving and hopefully exceeding the coach's own achievements.
5. The coach's reward comes from seeing the pupil's performance improve, rather than personally being able to perform the tasks.
6. The pupil's public may not be aware of the coach's role, but those 'in the know' recognize and acclaim the coach's contribution.

MANAGERS AS COACHES

The concept of the 'coach' parallels the role of the new generation of managers. As you adopt a coaching approach, you can expect a number of changes.

First, your people will learn to develop their own talents and abilities and to put them to good use, both for the organization, their teams and themselves. Second, when they are able to do this, you can expect your department to find a renewed energy – to function better, and to become a more exciting and enjoyable place in which to work. You will be

Coaching is part of the new approach to management.

able to take pleasure in these developments and they will reflect well on you.

Third, in sharing responsibility with your people you can expect to become less burdened yourself. You can have more time and energy available to move beyond just coping with problems. Perhaps you will be able to tackle more fundamentally important issues, or find time for a more balanced life in your work and outside work. Fourth, as your people develop their coaching skills in turn, these benefits will pass down the line to others, and then reflect back up the line to you.

COACHES AND PUPILS

As we have seen, coaching is an activity that takes place between a coach and a pupil. In this book I shall use the word 'pupil' to refer to the person being coached. This word can have connotations of inferiority or juniority. In the coaching context this is not so. Torvill and Dean were pupils of their coach but this does not mark them out as inferior or junior. Even the most senior managers can benefit from being pupil to a good coach.

APPROACHES TO LEARNING

HELPING PEOPLE TO LEARN

In the introductory book to this series, *Sharpen your skills in motivating people to perform*, Trevor Bentley describes what helps in effective learning. He describes the different ways people learn, the importance of continuous learning, a learning environment, and support for the learning process.

How we learnt ourselves may not be the most effective way.

There are many different ways of learning and each of us will have our preferences. My formative school education was in the 1950s and 1960s, and the emphasis was on the imparting of information, or 'informed learning'. It was natural for me to assume that this is the way one learns and to rely on giving lectures and presentations myself, which I did for many years. Since that time there has been recognition that the most effective learning takes place when there is a greater emphasis on exploration and experimentation. If we restrict people to a particular way of learning then we may restrict their learning.

The different ways of learning can be grouped into four main styles:

- informed learning
- experiential learning
- exploratory learning
- analytical learning.

The most effective learning takes place when we use a combination of these styles. Those of us who would help others to learn, whether we be managers or trainers, will be most effective when we support our pupils in their natural learning process, rather than impose a particular teaching style upon them.

Pupils learn best the way that suits them.

PUPIL-CENTRED LEARNING

The learning process must be centred on the needs of the pupil rather than on the needs of the coach. This may sound obvious, but it requires discipline on the part of the coaches, trainers or managers to put their own needs to one side in the interests of their pupils.

As a manager, for example, I may feel good at knowing the answers, being able to demonstrate superior skills and show competence in a subject. This, after all, confirms why I am the manager. However, for the pupil this can engender feelings of inferiority, incompetence and subordination – all factors that may detract from the most effective learning process.

In coaching, pupils' needs are paramount.

The challenge for managers is to make their skills available as a resource to pupils, rather than as a display of superiority.

HELPING YOUR PEOPLE BECOME COACHES

This book is not just about learning the coaching approach yourself, but about helping your people to become coaches in turn.

Being coached yourself contributes to your skill as a coach.

The single most effective way in which you can help your people become good coaches is to become one yourself. As your people experience the benefits of your coaching, so they will absorb the experience and use it in their practice. Your example will both give them both permission to adopt the coaching approach and a good lead to follow.

This book is also a resource to enable you to help your people develop their skills in coaching. Many of the structures and exercises are intended to be used with or by your people. So that the book can be used by your people as well as yourself, I have chosen to address it to the individual learning a topic or skill, rather than to someone teaching others. As you share your coaching skills and this book with your people, so they too can learn the coaching approach.

You can also use the skills that you are learning to coach your people in *their* coaching skills. Additionally, many of the exercises in the book involve working with others to support them in developing their skills – also an informal form of coaching.

THE IMPORTANCE OF MISTAKES

One of the most important steps in learning is the making of mistakes. It is by falling off a bicycle that we learn about balance. It is the role of the supportive manager to help the pupil in exploring, taking risks and making mistakes. When the pupil makes a mistake, as we all do at times, the supportive manager is there to help the pupil learn from the experience and find a better way.

Mistakes are great opportunities for learning.

Of course, it is also the task of the manager to keep an eye on pupils and to make sure that the situation is safe enough for their mistakes not to be catastrophic. When learning on the high wire, a safety net is necessary so that the risks can be taken safely. The manager who puts pupils unsupported into a situation where a mistake would be serious for the pupils or the organization is doing nobody a service. On the other hand, the manager who is over-protective and never gives pupils enough responsibility may inhibit the pupils' learning process. Their potential may be lost both for them and the organization.

The supportive learning environment is one in which it is safe enough to have a go, to make mistakes without fear of criticism, to learn, and to have another go.

THE LEARNING CYCLE

In preparing this book I have endeavoured to provide flexibility in learning possibilities by supporting the following learning pattern, although it has not always been possible to provide each element at each step.

1. *Input* You will be introduced to the subject matter and given information about it.
2. *Developing understanding* You will be given exercises or structures to develop your own or your people's understanding.
3. *Example* You will be given an example of the skills being used.
4. *Practice* You will be encouraged to develop your skills further through continuing practice.

INTRODUCING ROWENA AND HER TEAM

So that you have an example of how to apply the skills presented, you will be meeting Rowena and her team at various times in the book.

Rowena works for a company that publishes a number of magazines and specialist newspapers. Her boss, John, is Director of Local Government Publishing within the company. Rowena herself is manager of a monthly news magazine for local government.

Rowena's team includes Brian, the magazine editor, Mike who is in charge of production, Juliet who looks after advertising, Corrie who is in charge of circulation, and Pierre who is responsible for financial matters.

Rowena is seeking to introduce the coaching approach in

her work. You can follow her as she applies the skills presented in this book. In the interests of readability the pace in the dialogues is sometimes faster than it might be in practice.

HOW TO USE THIS BOOK

I intend you to be able to use your learning from this book step by step. It is not necessary to read and master all the material presented before you start to coach. I provide early on the material you need in order to start. In this way you can quickly gain benefit in your practice as a manager.

Subsequent chapters then help you develop your coaching skills in more depth. You can absorb these at your own pace and as fits with your work situation. By developing, refining and honing your coaching skills, you can expect to gain greater benefit and satisfaction through your coaching.

In Part One of the book I invite you to prepare the ground. By exploring the values and beliefs of coaching, and by involving your people in this process, you will be establishing or further developing a culture that supports the coaching approach.

Part Two introduces the idea of superior coaching – coaching that is not haphazard but a disciplined skill that achieves superior results (Kinlaw, 1996). You will learn about the values and discipline needed for superior coaching, and be shown how to hold superior coaching sessions. Having worked through to the end of this part, you can begin to apply coaching in your work practice.

In Part Three I return to the core skills of coaching and present them afresh, in more depth. I contend that you can only fully develop these skills in parallel with the continuing practice of coaching as established in Part Two.

When you feel comfortable with these core skills, you may want to develop your practice still further. In Part Four you will find material to develop your coaching skills to an advanced level. You can take these advanced topics one at a time, as few or as many as you wish. I regard the material in

Part Four as essential for those who want to develop their skills to a professional level, e.g. to work primarily as a coach rather than as a manager who uses coaching skills.

Use this book as you will. Enjoy it, enjoy your coaching, and enjoy watching your people develop their skills!

PREPARING THE GROUND

PART 1

In this part of the book you will be invited to prepare the ground for introducing the coaching approach into your work as a manager.

KEY LEARNING POINTS

You will have the opportunity to learn:

- that all managers have a distinctive style
- about your style and those of your people
- how to involve your people in the process of adopting the coaching approach
- about the existing coaching skills you and your people already have
- about potential difficulties you may encounter and the importance of addressing them

I presume that you are reading this book because you are taking the initiative to explore or further develop the coaching approach to management.

A new initiative is like a young plant that has potential but that takes time to develop its roots and become established. In the early stages it needs careful nurturing if it is to survive. Later, as it becomes better established, the plant is more able to withstand any difficulties that it meets. Sometimes new initiatives do not succeed. Often this is because insufficient attention has been given to preparing the ground. This process is so important that I shall devote the first part of this book to this process.

First, you will have the opportunity to look at the existing management styles within your organization and with which you and your colleagues are familiar. Then we shall look at the management values necessary to nurture the coaching approach, and compare these with your organization's existing styles. Finally, you will be invited to prepare the ground by involving your people in developing the coaching approach.

CHAPTER 2

Discovering your management style

The style is the man himself.

(Georges Buffon, *Discourse on his reception into the French Academy* (1750)

KEY LEARNING POINTS

In this chapter you will have the opportunity to learn about:

■ varying styles of management
■ your own favoured style
■ your colleagues' style
■ your colleagues' view of your style

INTRODUCTION

All managers have individual styles of management, which they have developed over the years. Your style will certainly have been influenced by your early life experiences and then

15

by your formal education. After that it will have been enriched through your experiences during your working life so far – some of which will have been good, some less so, and some perhaps plain difficult.

Thus each of us will have developed a style that draws on our mix of experiences. A painter's palette contains a selection of colours that the painter favours and from which he or she works. Some of us, consciously or otherwise, favour certain styles more than others, and the repertoire on our palettes will reflect this.

We all have personal styles of management.

If I fill my painting palette with my favourite greens, I can be very adept at green landscapes. But I may find it difficult to paint a fiery sunset, or an inner city scene. It is, therefore, important for us to check that we do have a palette suitable for the scene before us. Using the palette we have to hand rather than the right one for the job can be a serious handicap.

A palette has many different dimensions – the colour tint, hue, saturation, paint medium, texture, etc. Management styles, too, can be seen in many different dimensions. For our present purpose we shall consider one particularly relevant to coaching.

CHECKING YOUR MANAGEMENT STYLE

The following exercise can help you explore the aspects of your management style relevant to coaching. Be as honest with yourself as you can, and resist the natural tendency to respond as you would like to think things are. This is not a test. There are no right or wrong answers. The exercise is intended to be a stimulus for personal reflection and discussion. Take ten minutes or so to complete Exercise 1 now, before reading further.

Exercise 1 – Styles of management

Here are ten pairs of statements. Assign to each statement a weight from 0 to 10 which shows the relative strength of your belief in that statement (0=the weakest; 10=the strongest). The weights assigned must total 10 for each pair.

1. It is only human nature for people to do as little
   work as they can get away with. _____ (a)
   When people avoid work it is usually because their
   work has been deprived of its meaning. _____ (b)

   10

2. If employees have access to any information they
   want, they tend to have better attitudes and behave
   more responsibly. _____ (c)
   If employees have access to more information than
   they need to do their immediate tasks, they will
   usually misuse it. _____ (d)

   10

3. One problem in asking for the ideas of employees
   is that their perspective is too limited for their
   suggestions to be of much practical use. _____ (e)
   Asking employees for their ideas broadens their
   perspectives and results in the development of
   useful suggestions. _____ (f)

   10

4. If people don't use much imagination and ingenuity,
   it is probably because relatively few people have
   much of either. _____ (g)
   Most people are imaginative and creative but may
   not show it because of limitations imposed by
   supervision and the job. _____ (h)

   10

5. People tend to raise their standards if they are
   accountable for their own behaviour and for
   correcting their own mistakes. _____ (i)
   People tend to lower their standards if they are not
   punished for their misbehaviour and mistakes. _____ (j)

   10

6. It is better to give people both good and bad news
   because most employees want the whole story,
   no matter how painful. _____ (k)
   It is better to withhold unfavourable news about
   business because most employees really want to hear
   only the good news. _____ (l)

   10

17

7. Because a supervisor is entitled to more respect than those below him in the organization, it weakens his prestige to admit that a subordinate was right and he was wrong. ___ (m)

    Because people at all levels are entitled to equal respect, a supervisor's prestige is increased when he supports this principle by admitting that a subordinate was right and he was wrong. ___ (n)

    10

8. If you give people enough money, they are less likely to be concerned with such intangibles as responsibility and recognition. ___ (o)

    If you give people interesting and challenging work, they are less likely to complain about such things as pay and supplemental benefits. ___ (p)

    10

9. If people are allowed to set their own goals and standards of performance, they tend to set them higher than the boss would. ___ (q)

    If people are allowed to set their own goals and standards of performance, they tend to set them lower than the boss would. ___ (r)

    10

10. The more knowledge and freedom a person has regarding his job, the more controls are needed to keep him in line. ___ (s)

    The more knowledge and freedom a person has regarding his job, the fewer controls are needed to ensure satisfactory job performance. ___ (t)

    10

Now add up the weightings in two groups to get totals X and Y:

X = (a) + (d) + (e) + (g) + (j) + (l) + (m) + (o) + (r) + (s)
Y = (b) + (c) + (f) + (h) + (I) + (k) + (n) + (p) + (q) + (t)

This exercise is adapted from Scott Myers (1970), and is reproduced with permission.

This exercise is a development of the ideas of Douglas McGregor (1960), who described two ends of a continuum of management assumptions. He labelled the traditional assumptions about the need for direction as Theory X, and the emerging assumptions about people's self-motivation and desire to improve themselves as Theory Y. In practice, every manager's personal style will lie somewhere between these two extremes, and your score in this exercise allows you to assess the balance in your management style between Theories X and Y.

Coaching builds on people's self-motivation and desire to improve themselves. If your style is towards Theory Y you are well placed to work with your people in developing a coaching approach.

If you are a Theory X person, on the other hand, it may be that your interest in coaching is an important step in developing a Theory Y dimension to your style. If you feel unsympathetic to the Theory Y view, you should think carefully – it may not be the appropriate time for you to take a lead in introducing the coaching approach. Either way, it may be helpful for you to work further in developing your understanding and approach to working with people.

YOUR VIEWS OF YOUR COLLEAGUES

You may find it interesting to complete Exercise 1 as if on behalf of your colleagues, for example as you experience them. Include your subordinates and your boss. Then consider how your perception of their styles differs from your perception of your own.

As your colleagues work through these exercises they too

will complete this exercise for themselves and, perhaps, as they see you. If you and they are willing, it can be helpful to share your perceptions of each other.

How others see you and how you see yourself may be different.

This sharing may confirm what you already know, which can be reassuring. Sometimes someone else's perception of your style can be different from your own. This is not an issue of who is right and who is wrong. Rather it suggests that some people perceive your style differently from how you perceive it yourself. Becoming aware of how differently others perceive you can be helpful when you get unexpected reactions. If there is a consistent difference between other people's views and your own view of your style, you may want to reflect on why this is.

ACTION LIST

1. Complete Exercise 1 and reflect on your own style of management.
2. Reflect on your colleagues' styles of management.
3. Invite your colleagues also to complete actions 1 and 2 above.
4. Meet together and share your findings and views of each other.

CHAPTER 3

INVOLVING YOUR PEOPLE

The real leader has no need to lead – he is content to point the way.

Henry Miller, *The Wisdom of the Heart* (1941)

KEY LEARNING POINTS

In this chapter you will be encouraged to:

- involve your manager in your introduction of coaching
- involve your people
- explore with them the changing role of management
- give feedback to each other on existing coaching skills
- discover the 'pros and cons' of adopting coaching

INTRODUCTION

Coaching is not an activity you can do alone. Inevitably it involves others, but this involvement is not just with pupils. Part of learning together is involving others, not just as pupils but in the whole process of developing a coaching culture.

The most effective way of establishing this as normal

procedure is by involving other people as you introduce the coaching approach.

INVOLVING YOUR OWN MANAGER

As you introduce and develop the coaching approach, you will hopefully have the support of your own manager. Ideally your manager will be actively supporting this process, and perhaps coaching you. It is particularly helpful if you can experience the coaching process yourself. If you have not already done so, arrange to talk to your manager about your initiative. Find out how sympathetic he or she is, and how much support you will have.

Involve your manager and get his or her support.

If your manager is supportive, make good use of this. Involve him or her in the process of preparing the ground, described in this part of the book. Encourage your manager to study this book. Arrange for coaching sessions for yourself in the work of introducing the coaching approach.

If your manager is unsympathetic, or does not have the time to support you in this way, I recommend that you find the necessary support from somewhere else. Perhaps there is someone who could act as an honorary uncle or aunt for you in this respect, or you could make an arrangement with one of your peers. Some managers go outside their organization and obtain this support from a professional management coach or mentor.

Be sure you have support from somewhere.

INVOLVING YOUR OWN PEOPLE

Coaching is a two-way process, and not something that is 'done to' someone. It is, therefore, important to talk things over with your people, perhaps in a team meeting, and to engage their interest.

Most initiatives that fail or run out of steam do so because the ground has not been adequately prepared and, in particular, because others have not been sufficiently involved at an early stage. When people are included early, they can

Involving others early on is very important.

'buy in' to the initiative and support it even when the going may be hard.

You can explain that you want to develop a coaching approach to support them in their work, and that you would also like to support them in developing this approach with their people.

Your initiative may be welcomed, or it may be met with concern, as proposed changes often are. You may get a mixed reaction from the same people, or from different people.

It is good to have a reaction, even when it is less than positive. This is an indication that what you have said is being taken seriously. When you know what problems people see, then you can work with them. Silence or a lack of interest may indicate that you have not been heard clearly, or that you and your people have not been engaged in the subject sufficiently.

Even a bad reaction is better than no reaction at all.

In the following sections I offer some structures to help you focus your discussions and to come to some understanding with your people about what you and they are expecting from coaching.

THE CHANGING JOB OF LEADING AND MANAGING

The job of leading and managing people has changed significantly over the last 10 years or so. You can use Exercise 2 to explore with your team how they and you see these changes.

Exercise 2 – Exploring the changing role of managers

The role of managers and leaders has changed significantly in the last 10 years or so.

1. Work individually and think about these changes. In the first column below jot down a few notes about what you believe managers and leaders are doing less of than they were. In the

second column jot down some notes about what they are doing more of today.

Doing less of...	Doing more of...

2. Now come together as a group and discuss what each person has noted. Identify those points that your team feel are the most significant and important ways in which the role of manager and leader has changed.

FEEDBACK ON EXISTING COACHING SKILLS

In following this book you are showing your people how to develop their coaching skills by sharing with them how you develop your own.

As you and they embark on developing skills, it will be helpful to know from where you are starting – the extent of your existing coaching skills. The most reliable guide is how others currently perceive you in this respect. Exercise 3 provides a structure in which you and your team can give feedback to each other on your present skills. What is important is learning about yourself from the feedback, rather than the actual numbers generated.

Feedback is often most helpful when you can receive it without needing to get into discussion about it or trying to justify your position. If there are any surprises for you, I suggest you just reflect on what you are being offered and try to notice any common patterns among the different commentators in particular.

Help each other learn about your existing coaching skills.

Exercise 3 – Coaching skills feedback

Arrange for four or five of your colleagues (and this can include your boss and subordinates) to complete the following questionnaire indicating how they see you. They should then pass the completed form back to you.

Name of person I am evaluating: ....

To what degree do you believe the following statements are true for this person? Circle the numbers that best apply.

Key: 1 = very characteristic   2 = moderately characteristic
       3 = somewhat characteristic   4 = moderately uncharacteristic
       5 = very uncharacteristic

In relationships with employees and co-workers:

	High				Low
1. Shows co-workers that he/she believes they want to be fully competent in their jobs.	1	2	3	4	5
2. Gives co-workers the chance to demonstrate their competence.	1	2	3	4	5
3. Encourages co-workers to take on more challenging tasks.	1	2	3	4	5
4. Makes minimum use of controls to manage co-workers' performance.	1	2	3	4	5
5. Is quick to express appreciation for co-workers' good work.	1	2	3	4	5
6. Gives co-workers every opportunity to improve when they make mistakes.	1	2	3	4	5
7. Make sure work of co-workers is as challenging as he/she can make it.	1	2	3	4	5
8. Is easily available to talk to about improving performance.	1	2	3	4	5
9. Makes it easy for co-workers to tell him/her they don't know how to do something.	1	2	3	4	5
10. Often initiates conversations to help co-workers perform at their top potential.	1	2	3	4	5

YOUR 'PROS AND CONS' OF COACHING

Developing the coaching approach will have advantages for both you and your people. You can expect some disadvantages too. It is important to identify what you think these are.

It is only when you are convinced of the advantages and have addressed the disadvantages that you will invest the required energy and time. The same is also true for your people, and indeed for your manager. Exercise 5 later in this section will help you to do this with your people. However, before others can take part in this they need to have an idea of what coaching is about. You can use Exercise 4 to help them establish this.

Exercise 4 – What is coaching?

This exercise can help develop an understanding of what coaching is about.

1. Think of a coach as someone who periodically has conversations with others and is able to help them improve their performance by teaching them new skills, helping them solve problems or challenging them to take on more difficult tasks and jobs.
2. Work individually for five minutes and think about the best coach that you can remember from your work experience. Jot down a few notes about why you remember the person as such a good coach.
3. Work as a team and appoint a recorder. Discuss what each person has noted from step 2. Develop a profile of what your team thinks a good coach does.

Now you can use the following 'brainstorming' Exercise 5 to help you identify the 'pros and cons' of adopting the coaching approach in your organization or department. If you are not familiar with brainstorming, first read Appendix 1.

You can do this exercise in a meeting with your people. Alternatively, it may feel more appropriate if you invite them to prepare their ideas in their own peer groupings.

Now review this output with your people. You need to get a feel for the balance of energy for or against the initiative. It is most important that you attend to any potential problems that may work against the success of the initiative.

Find out about any problems your people see in coaching now, rather than later.

Exercise 5 – Your 'pros and cons' of coaching

Arrange for a brainstorming of the 'pros and cons' of developing a coaching approach. This should be done by three separate groups:

1. yourself, perhaps together with your peer managers,
2. your people,
3. your own manager, perhaps together with his or her peers.

Each group should end up with a comparative list, like this:

Advantages	Disadvantages

Now meet to collate and summarize your output as follows:

Viewed by	Advantages	Disadvantages
Your manager		
Yourself		
Your people		

Discuss this summary.
What actions can you take to address the disadvantages?

ROWENA CHECKS OUT HOW COACHING IS VIEWED

Rowena has talked to her boss John about her ideas of developing a coaching approach. He has made supportive noises but she is still unsure what he really thinks. She therefore asks him for his 'pros and cons'. She then raises the idea with her people at their regular meeting. There is rather a mixed reaction but considerable interest. Rowena decides to invite her people to brainstorm their 'pros and cons' collectively with her, but identifies her own views by using a different coloured pen. Then Brian, her production manager, collates and summarizes the various inputs:

Viewed by	Advantages	Disadvantages
John (Rowena's manager)	Spread Rowena's skills into team Team likely to be better motivated	Potential disruption to already tight schedules When are they going to find time?
Rowena	Team more involved Team better motivated Broader spread for worries	Take more time Slower actions Less control over how things done Concern at less control over critical work Feel less responsible for outcomes
Rowena's team	More involved in decision making More involved in deciding how to deal with problems Opportunity to develop own skills More responsibility	Used to knowing what is to be done Will take more time, which is already under pressure When would we be coached?

In reviewing this outcome Rowena realizes that availability of time is a common concern. It will be necessary to schedule coaching development activities so they do not jeopardize critical activities and the monthly reporting cycle in particular. When she shares this realization with her people there is an immediate recognition of how crucial availability of time would be, and relief that this has been recognized.

Rowena also realizes that she has been somewhat ambivalent about adopting the coaching style as she felt it might diminish her kudos and recognition. She decides to talk this over with John and sound out how he would view her competency if she were less directive with her people.

In talking this through with John later she discovers that he is rather concerned at Rowena's workload, and he feels that she might benefit from delegating more. John reckons some of Rowena's people have real potential, but are rather 'under her shadow'. He encourages Rowena to follow the coaching angle, and feels the initiative will probably do her credit. They agree that they will review this aspect in six months and that John will let her know then if he feels she is compromising her position.

ACTION LIST

1. Talk with your own manager about your plans to develop the coaching approach.
2. Set up a discussion with your people about coaching.
3. Explore with them the changing role of management, using Exercise 2.
4. Explore with your people how your own and their coaching skills are currently perceived by others, using Exercise 3.
5. Develop as a group your understanding of the advantages and disadvantages of the coaching approach. You can use Exercise 5.
6. Identify with your people actions to address any concerns about the coaching approach, and act on them.

SUPERIOR
COACHING

PART 2

In this part of the book we will learn about coaching – not just any coaching but *superior coaching*, and you will be guided in starting to coach.

KEY LEARNING POINTS

The following are the key learning points that will be covered in the four chapters in this part:

- the concept of superior coaching
- the values and characteristics of superior coaching
- the core skills used in superior coaching
- how to shape a coaching session
- how to start coaching

Anyone can presume to coach – that is, anyone can initiate conversations with co-workers with the intention of helping them improve their performance. If the coach is not clear how to conduct a coaching session or what he or she is trying to achieve, the results will be random and unpredictable. Useful results may be achieved now and again, but only by chance.

Coaching carries enormous potential to help individuals and teams achieve superior performance as well as greater job satisfaction. It is too important to leave this to chance – to use it without serious preparation and skill development.

Much coaching largely fails to have an impact on performance because people who try to coach have not developed a clear picture in their minds of what coaching involves. They have not grasped its essential characteristics and shape.

In this part of the book I will introduce you to *superior coaching* – coaching that is disciplined and structured to achieve a continuous improvement in performance (Kinlaw, 1996). You will learn the skills necessary to conduct superior coaching sessions and to start integrating them into your management practice.

In subsequent parts of the book I return to explore the coaching skills in more depth, so that you can develop and hone your practice to make it even more effective.

CHAPTER 4

COACHING VALUES

AND

CHARACTERISTICS

A man who doesn't trust himself can never really trust anyone else.

Cardinal de Retz, *Mémoires* (1718)

KEY LEARNING POINTS

In this chapter you will have the opportunity to learn about:

■ superior coaching
■ particular core values shared by superior coaches
■ the characteristics of superior coaching
■ how to explore and develop these values and characteristics

INTRODUCTION

The coaching approach builds on certain assumptions regarding human behaviour and motivation. In this chapter you will learn about these core values and the coaching approach to learning. You will have the opportunity to check out your own assumptions and values.

For coaching to be effective it is important that the coach hold the values and beliefs that support the coaching process, and that pupils know this through their experience of the coach. Studies have shown that when it comes to communicating non-factual things, such as values and attitudes, the words we speak play only a minor part in the process. The most influential aspects of such communication are non-verbal (Table 4.1).

TABLE 4.1: Dimensions of non-factual communication

7%	comes through the words spoken
38%	comes through the voice, tone, rate and inflection
53%	is through face and body

So the majority of the communication is unconscious and not something that can be 'managed'. If the coach does not believe in the values being espoused, this will communicate itself somehow. If the coach says one thing but believes another, pupils will receive mixed messages. They are unlikely to be sufficiently conscious of what is happening or confident enough to challenge this. Instead they will feel confused or unconvinced, and so the coaching remains ineffective or even counterproductive.

If we say one thing but believe something else, we give mixed and confusing messages.

CORE VALUES

In Chapter 3 you were invited to explore with your colleagues your present attitudes relevant to coaching. Coaching depends upon the coach holding certain core values that support the coaching process. In this section we shall explore these core values.

First take five minutes now to do Exercise 6, either by yourself or as a brainstorm in a group.

Exercise 6 – Values and beliefs for coaching

Develop a list of the values and beliefs that you feel will support the coaching process. Consider the following dimensions:

- values and beliefs of the coach;
- values and beliefs of the pupil;
- values and beliefs within the organization.

You can compare your list of values and beliefs with the list developed by Kinlaw (1996), which is reproduced in Appendix 2.

In coaching the coach helps pupils develop their abilities and competency. This raises the question of whether people always have competency to develop. It is now becoming recognized that one of the distinguishing features of humankind is the extraordinary innate competency in all of us.

Many of us, however, have experiences that deny our competency. We may have been told we are stupid or lazy or incompetent by those in authority. Some believe this and seem to become what they are told they are. Many reject these judgements and yet in some way retain a doubt. Sometimes we may even choose to view others as incompetent as a means of distancing ourselves from our doubts about our own competency.

Coaches need to believe in human competency.

Superior coaches believe that people are innately competent. This does not mean that everybody is equally skilled or clever, nor does it preclude people using their competency in ways that may be damaging. It does recognize that people want to be competent and, given the necessary help, will strive to become more competent. Superior coaches believe that their pupils gain satisfaction from their competency and must be given the opportunity to demonstrate it on a continual basis.

Coaches need to believe that people strive for achievement.

Superior coaches also recognize the basic human desire to achieve. This does not imply that everybody can or wants to achieve the same things. Different people strive in different ways. One may want to achieve high office; another may want to achieve a comfortable life. Both can strive for that achievement. It is the role of the coach to support pupils in a natural desire to achieve their work goals.

On this basis, managing people by control or coercion denies their desire for achievement and does not support or encourage them to improve their performance to the benefit of their work. It can even subvert people's achievements towards doing the minimum or looking after their own needs. Either of these is to the detriment of the organization.

Superior performance comes about when people and the teams they comprise are committed to perform at the best of their ability. In order for people to be committed, they must:

- understand what they are doing and why it is important;
- have the competencies to perform the jobs that are expected of them;
- feel appreciated for what they do;
- feel challenged by their jobs;
- have the chance to improve when they make mistakes.

Superior coaches share the values of human competency and the human striving for achievement. They also understand the importance of coaching conversations, whether they be informal exchanges or a formal session. They use their interactions with individuals and teams as a potential opportunity to coach – rather than to direct.

Coaching builds on pupils' natural competence and ability.

Superior coaches also bring discipline and a developed set of their own skills to their coaching activity. Superior coaches:

1. Believe that they must initiate coaching interactions and use every interaction with individuals and teams as a potential opportunity to coach – rather than to direct.
2. Believe in discipline, and view coaching as a set of competencies that they can learn and test like any other set of skills required for managing and leading.

CHARACTERISTICS OF SUPERIOR COACHING

Positive results from coaching interactions depend on the coach:

1. Creating the essential conditions that support superior coaching.
2. Employing the critical skills for superior coaching.
3. Being disciplined enough to create the structure of the core coaching conversation that underlies superior coaching.
4. Being able to apply the skills and core conversation in a way that achieves improved performance.

The logic is that superior coaches move from their internal set of values into learning all that it takes to be a superior coach. They develop the essential characteristics and learn to use the critical skills. They learn to create the core conversation in coaching opportunities.

Superior coaching is not haphazard but disciplined.

Five definite characteristics distinguish superior coaching from other such conversations. These are:

1. balance
2. being concrete
3. shared responsibility
4. respect
5. shape.

In the rest of this chapter you will have the opportunity to explore these characteristics further. If you are using this book to develop your people's coaching skills it will be helpful if you do the exercises with them as a team. Alternatively you may wish to get together with some of your colleagues for this purpose.

Some of these exercises involve giving feedback. There is some advice about giving feedback in Appendix 3.

BALANCE

Superior coaches maintain a balance of input between coach and pupil.

Superior coaching is not one-sided. There is exchange, a questioning and sharing of information and ideas with the full involvement of all parties. A superior coach creates balance in the coaching interaction. In some conversations it will be the coach who does most of the initiating but in others it will be the person being coached.

You can use Exercise 7 to explore with your people how to create balance in a coaching interaction.

Exercise 7 – Creating balance

Creating balance is important in a coaching session. Working as a team, identify and record as many ways as you can of:

1. Creating *imbalance*, for example the coach does too much talking.
2. Creating *balance*, for example both coach and pupil contribute to the conversation.

Discuss your findings and consider the effect of imbalance and balance on the coaching interaction.

BEING CONCRETE

Another characteristic of superior coaching is that it focuses on what the pupil can improve. The coach uses language that is to the point and encourages the pupil to be specific. It is pointless, for example, to try to help someone be more conscientious or a better team player unless we are clear what sort of improvement we are seeking. Only when both coach and pupil understand what improvement they desire can the pupil improve performance.

Use Exercise 8 to develop skills in being concrete.

Superior coaches avoid generalizations and are specific. They encourage their pupils to be specific.

Exercise 8 – Being concrete

1. Each member of the team selects from the following list one coaching opportunity for which he or she would like to make a concrete statement as a coach to his or her fellow team members.
   - Describe to your team at least one way in which it could improve its performance.
   - Describe to your team what you think are the two most important characteristics of superior teams.
   - Describe to your team what you think is the most

important skill in being a superior coach.
- Describe to your team what you think are the team's strengths.
2. Each team member prepares their statements.

Read steps 3 and 4 before continuing because they take place together.

3. Each person reads to the team his or her statement from step 2, after which each team member gives feedback based on the following questions:
   - What part of the statement was clearly concrete, i.e. immediately understood?
   - What part of the statement was insufficiently concrete, i.e. not immediately understood?
   - What should the person change to make the statement more concrete ?
4. After the team member has received feedback from each person, he or she should indicate how the *feedback* could be more concrete, i.e. immediately understood.
5. Discuss your experiences in this exercise.

SHARED RESPONSIBILITY

Superior coaches share responsibility for effective outcomes with their pupils.

Both the coach and pupil have a shared responsibility to work together for the continuous improvement of performance. All participants in a coaching conversation share the responsibility for making that conversation as useful as possible, and for the continuous performance that follows the conversation.

Develop skills in sharing responsibility using Exercise 9.

Exercise 9 – Practising shared responsibility

Use this exercise to develop team members' ability to find balance in sharing responsibility in coaching interactions.

1. Assign the following mini-cases to team members in order. If the team is large, assign more than one person to the same case. Alternatively, you might use scenarios from your working situation. Members then prepare something they might say during the coaching interaction described which would help develop the proper degree of shared responsibility with the other person(s).

2. Each person reads his or her statement from step 1 to the team. The team then gives feedback around the following questions :
   - Did the coach communicate a sense of shared responsibility?
   - Did the coach assume too much responsibility?
   - Did the coach try to give the other person(s) too much responsibility?
   - How might the statement that the coach made be improved?

   When you receive feedback from your colleagues, you do not have to accept it, but try to use it. Avoid trying to justify what you originally said.
3. Discuss your experience of this exercise.

Mini cases for Exercise 9

Case A

> You have an employee who persistently makes grammatical mistakes in written reports. The employee is working on a report analysing plans for office automation. You have reviewed a draft and found several incomplete sentences, non-agreement in subjects and verbs, and mistakes in punctuation. You have called the employee in to discuss the problem.

Case B

> You have stopped by the office of one of your people, as part of your 'walking around' strategy. You ask the employee, 'How are things going?' The employee says 'I don't think I am going to meet the planned schedule for the next design review.'

Case C

> The results of a recent organizational survey show that the people in your work group have a low commitment to doing their best all the time. You have called a team meeting to discuss the problem.

Case D

> Your work group is required to submit weekly notes
> describing major activities, problems and achievements to
> senior management. You have an employee who regularly
> fails to prepare those notes on time. You are in the midst of
> a coaching conversation to address the employee's
> performance.

Case E

> You have an employee who never volunteers for tough or
> dirty jobs, and rarely assists other work group members
> when they need help. Others' impressions are that the
> employee is willing to do only the minimum amount of work
> to get by and has little commitment to doing superior work.
> You are discussing the problem with the employee.

RESPECT

Superior coaches respect the pupils they are coaching. What is
more, they demonstrate this respect in their attitude to their
pupils. In this context, respect implies that you accept pupils'
abilities and good intentions, and do not imply or infer that
they are stupid, inferior or evil. It is about involving the other
person in a way that makes them a fully accepted player. You
can use the following Exercise 10 to practise establishing
respect.

**Superior coaches respect
their pupils' abilities and
communicate this to them.**

Exercise 10 – Establishing respect

You can do this exercise working in a team or as individuals.

1. Identify a coaching scenario, either from your own experience
   or a fictitious one, such as from the mini cases for Exercise 9.
   If you are working in a group, you may wish to avoid using a
   real scenario with someone known to the others unless there
   is a high degree of trust among you.
2. Imagine you are discussing the scenario with the person
   concerned. Place an empty chair opposite you in which you
   can imagine that person sitting.

3. Identify (perhaps by recording or speaking) what you might say to the person that demonstrates your *lack of respect* for him/her. Give yourself licence in this exercise to be as blunt and frank as you wish.
4. Now take the place of the person you have been addressing and occupy the same chair. Explore (and say to others present) how it feels to receive these comments. Consider how you would prefer the problem to have been addressed.
5. Return to your own role and chair, and now address the person respectfully about the same problem. Value the abilities he or she does have, the efforts that person does make, and involve him or her in dealing with the problem.

SHAPE

Superior coaching has a distinctive shape that you can follow over and over again. This is more apparent in a coaching session than in a brief interaction. It is easiest to practise establishing the discipline of shape in formal sessions, and then you will find you can give shape even to brief interactions. The session is shaped so that you can:

Superior coaches shape the coaching interaction so that it achieves an improvement in performance.

1. identify the goal of the conversation;
2. encourage the flow of conversation to expand the information available;
3. focus the participants as they move towards the goal.

Shaping a coaching conversation is crucial, and this will be discussed in more detail in Chapter 6.

ACTION LIST

1. Get together with your people as a group and decide on the core values of coaching, using Exercise 6.
2. As a group discover how you can create balance in a coaching interaction, using Exercise 7.
3. As a group practise being concrete, using Exercise 8.
4. As a group find a balance in taking shared responsibility, using Exercise 9.
5. Explore the issue of respect in coaching. Use Exercise 10, either alone or in the group.

CHAPTER 5

CORE SKILLS

'Tis skill, not strength, that governs a ship.

Thomas Fuller, *Gnomologia* (1732)

KEY LEARNING POINTS

In this chapter you will have the opportunity to:

- learn about the core skills of coaching
- practise these skills
- recognize these skills
- discover which of these skills you use

INTRODUCTION

There are certain core skills that are critical for the success of a coaching conversation. I will introduce them here, because you need them as you start your coaching practice. They are so central and important that I will be revisiting some of these skills again in Part Three of the book, when you will also have the opportunity to develop them in more depth.

The core skills are:

- active listening
- enquiring
- focusing

- teaching
- affirming

ACTIVE LISTENING

I am using the term *active listening* to describe a powerful and disciplined form of listening, which is a long way from most listening that is quite informal and casual. When we use active listening well, it can be an important and empowering experience for the person to whom we are listening. Superior coaches use active listening so that they can fully hear what the pupil needs to communicate and so that the pupil feels fully heard.

Active listening is not casual listening but a powerful discipline.

ATTENDING

The first condition for listening is for the coach to attend fully to the pupil. This can be done by:

- facing the other person;
- keeping comfortable eye contact ;
- acknowledging what is said;
- avoiding distracting behaviours such as fidgeting, thumbing through papers, or interrupting.

The vocal aspects of attending include all the grunts and groans that communicate to the other person that the coach is paying attention. These include such responses as 'uh huh', 'yes', 'I can see that', 'OK' and the like.

These acknowledgements indicate to the pupil that the coach is listening and, therefore, they encourage the pupil to interact easily and to develop the necessary information. They do not, of course, guarantee that the coach is actually listening. Coaching will be most effective when the coach really is giving full attention to the pupil.

LISTENING

The aim of listening is, put simply, to hear what is being said. This requires the listener to suspend judgement and not to start forming opinions. It means concentrating on understanding what the other person is trying to communicate rather than deciding if what the person is saying is right or wrong, or if you agree with it or not.

When coaches make premature judgements they disrupt the development of information and communicate lack of respect for the other person. This can destroy the shape of the superior coaching conversation. Coaches may do this by:

■ being too quick to reject what the pupil is trying to communicate;
■ being too quick to use their own beliefs and values to interpret what the pupil is trying to communicate;
■ thinking too much about what they want to say, rather than hearing what the pupil is trying to say;
■ being too quick to give irrelevant information not needed by the pupil or not needed to resolve the problem being discussed.

REFLECTING

Reflecting involves completing the 'listening loop' by making short summaries or paraphrases of what is being said. This confirms that we have heard correctly what has been said, and allows the speaker to move on to the next thought or topic.

Reflecting is not an opportunity for listeners to put their own slant on what has been said, or to slip in their view or opinion.

ENQUIRING

Enquiring helps pupils develop understanding.

The second core skill is enquiring. The key to superior coaching is to develop sufficient information so that pupils can discover how to improve their performance. Coaches can become skilled at knowing the sort of information that pupils need to know, without the coaches needing to know the answers themselves.

An example of such an enquiry might be: 'So what did you do when you learned the contractor was going to be late completing the first phase?'

FOCUSING

Focusing is a variation of enquiring which encourages pupils to identify what they need to do to make progress. It is not about manipulating pupils into doing what coaches want them to do, but about helping pupils explore their options or evaluate possible strategies.

Pupils need to focus on determining what actions to take.

'So you seem to have three alternative options here ... what are their pros and cons?'

'Which of these options do you favour?'

'So, if you are going to give the contractor an extension, how are you going to ensure there is no further slippage?'

TEACHING

Sometimes pupils may be having difficulty grasping a skill that the coach has. It can be most helpful for the coach to demonstrate the relevant skill, just as a sports coach might demonstrate a particular shot or move.

Coaches may usefully be able to teach pupils specific skills.

There may be many reasons why a coach teaches a pupil. Some are listed below but you may wish to add some of your own:

- The pupil has asked for help in learning a skill or grasping a point.
- It will be quicker for the coach to do it than wait for the pupil.
- It is easier to show than to explain.
- The pupil seems unable to find a solution without help.
- The coach is very adept at the task.
- The coach finds demonstrating very satisfying.

Consider which of these are centred on the needs of the pupil and which on the needs of the coach.

AFFIRMING

We all need affirmation in what we do. Affirming reinforces the sense of competency in a person and contributes directly

We all need affirming in what we do.

to that person's commitment to improve further. For many it is the fuel of motivation. When a coach affirms, this also demonstrates belief in the competency of the pupil.

Affirming during a coaching interaction may draw attention to the pupil's competence on the job, or competence in the coaching interaction.

It is important that the affirmation is genuine and given willingly by the coach, otherwise it can sound hollow or patronizing. Some people need to discover how to affirm others. Examples might be: 'The delays at the contractors have really complicated things. I appreciate the hard work you have put in to minimize the impact', or 'I note how well you have clarified your options during this session. You now have some clear actions to take.'

RECOGNIZING INTERVENTIONS

It will be helpful for you to listen in on some coaching or other management interactions, and to practise recognizing the basic skills being used. This will help you develop your awareness of types of intervention, and increase your choice of intervention.

This exercise may only be comfortable for your people if you are able to develop a strong sense of 'learning together'. It may be helpful if you first express your willingness for others to listen in on you and to address any reservations they have. Of course agreement also needs to be obtained from the relevant pupil or supervisee.

Exercise 11 is a tool to enable you to note which of the five core skills are being used.

Exercise 11 – Recognizing basic skills

Use this exercise to note the types of intervention being used in a management interaction. Place a mark in the column under Count each time you recognize one of the types. Write down a good example of each type used.

Type	Count	Example
Active listening		
Enquiring		
Focusing		
Teaching		
Affirming		

Do not expect all types to be used in every conversation you hear.

You may also find it helpful to get someone to make these observations on some of your conversations. You can then see which types of skill you use most frequently. If there are some skills you do not use, is this because they were not appropriate, or is it a skill that you need to develop?

ACTION LIST
1. Check that you understand the five core skills of coaching discussed in this chapter.
2. Arrange to listen in on some helping conversations. Using the form in Exercise 11, record the types of interventions that occur.
3. Arrange for a colleague to listen to some of your conversations and to note the types of intervention you use.
4. Reflect on the balance of intervention types used.

CHAPTER 6

THE SHAPE OF A COACHING SESSION

'Begin at the beginning,' the King said gravely, 'and go on till you come to the end; then stop'.

Lewis Carroll, *Alice's Adventures in Wonderland* (1865)

KEY LEARNING POINTS

In this chapter you will have the opportunity to learn about:

■ the shape of the superior coaching session
■ how to shape a session so that it achieves results
■ managing boundaries

INTRODUCTION

Coaching interactions can occur in many different circumstances – while you are walking around the job, in a corridor, at a computer terminal, in the canteen, or in a session set aside for the purpose.

Superior coaching sessions have a distinctive shape.

In this chapter we look at the structure of the coaching session, in which you set time aside specifically for coaching.

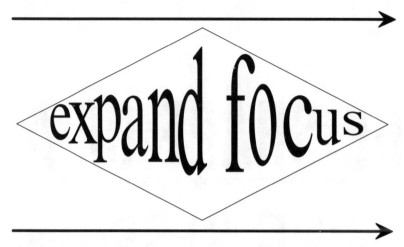

FIGURE 6.1: Outline shape of a coaching session

The superior coaching session has more than just a beginning and end; it has a distinctive shape. The session moves through clear phases. This helps both coach and pupil to orientate themselves and ensures an effective outcome. By following this shape, you can arrange your coaching sessions so that they develop and deliver effective outcomes.

A brief coaching interaction may not seem to have room for planned phases. However, once you are skilled at giving shape to formal sessions, you will naturally give some degree of shape to even brief coaching interactions.

We can imagine the shape of a coaching session, in outline, as shown in Figure 6.1. In the first half of the session we concentrate on expanding the pupil's awareness of the subject. In the second half we concentrate on focusing the pupil on what he or she needs to do to make progress and improve performance.

In practice each of these two phases contains sub-phases as follows:

1. Expanding
   - *Attending to the field*   Opening the session, creating space and boundaries, clearing clutter.
   - *Agreeing aims*   Agreeing what the session is about.
   - *Awareness*   Developing pupil and coach awareness of the issues.

2. Focusing
   - *Analysis*   Exploring the options.
   - *Action*   Agreeing or taking action, developing skills.
   - *Assessment*   Learning from the process.

THE PHASES IN DETAIL

We now explore each of the six phases of the coaching session. In practice there is often no sharp transition from one phase to the next, but rather a shift of emphasis.

We shall also follow Rowena as she shapes a coaching session with Pierre, her finance manager.

ATTENDING TO THE FIELD

Before we can hold a successful session, we need to create the right space for it. A busy office with other people milling around and perhaps overhearing the conversation is not conducive to concentration, nor may it be a safe space in which to explore openly any difficulties. Choosing an appropriate venue is clearly important. So also is the absence of interruptions.

Coaches need to create an appropriate space for coaching sessions.

It is also important that coach and pupil are aware of how long the session will be. If one party is anticipating a five-minute chat and the other is settling in for an hour, this will be confusing. If coach and pupil have different expectations, it will be necessary to reach an agreement. It is possible that you may need to revise this once you have established the aims of the session, but otherwise it is helpful to hold to the agreed duration of the session.

Rowena has had to rush back from a senior management briefing to meet with Pierre for their regular coaching session in her office.

Rowena   Hi Pierre … come on in!
Pierre   Thanks. I did wonder whether you would have time for me this morning.

Pierre is indicating that he is aware how rushed Rowena is. Perhaps he will be reluctant to raise any concerns he has under these circumstances. Rowena is aware that her secretary is not at her desk, that the phone is unattended and that the secretary may look in on her return. Even if these interruptions do not occur, Rowena may be wondering if they will. She decides to deal with them so she can attend to Pierre.

Rowena Just a minute … I need to ensure we are not disturbed. [She selects 'Do not Disturb' on the telephone.] Right, yes it's been rather hectic, but I am now here and ready for our session, and we have until 1:00pm.

Rowena now feels she can focus on Pierre and is free to give him time.

Pierre Look, if you are too busy, we could leave it until next time.

Rowena notices this is the second time Pierre has alluded to her 'busyness'. Is something troubling him? She decides to explore.

Rowena You seem very aware of how busy I must be.
Pierre Well, what with the briefing this morning, I imagine you may have things to do.
Rowena Such as …
Pierre Well, I don't know… I don't know what it was about.

Rowena realizes that there may be speculation about the briefing and Pierre may be worried about his position. In fact he is not directly affected, so she decides to clear his uncertainty.

Rowena I'll be briefing you all this afternoon, but for now I can say that there was nothing that directly affects us or your work.

Pierre looks relieved and visibly relaxes.

Issues 'present' for coach or pupil need either to be cleared or addressed in the session.

At the start of a meeting there may be many issues around. It is important to acknowledge what is on the mind of pupil or coach. They can then release or 'park' any matters that are not important to the session. If they do not deal with such matters adequately, they are likely to intrude on the minds of the participants and get in the way of an effective session.

Sometimes an intrusive issue may not dissolve itself in this way. In this case it needs to be dealt with as part of the session – indeed it may become the main focus.

AGREEING AIMS

Once coach and pupil have created the space for the session, it is important for them to agree on its aims. It is important for both coach and pupil to know what these are, and establishing them is the first objective. The session will normally focus on the pupil's needs. However, sometimes the coach may have a particular need and it is important that these are stated.

The aims for the session need to be established.

Otherwise the coach's aims are likely to intrude into the session in an indirect or manipulative way.

Occasionally a coaching session may be arranged in which the aims are not obvious. In that case the first task must be to establish what the needs are. Once the aims are established the coaching session can continue or, if more appropriate, a session can be agreed for another time.

Rowena	So ... how do you want to use today's session, Pierre?
Pierre	Well, there's the problem with variations in production costs, and how that is making it difficult for me to manage the cash flow. . . and there's the irregularity of advertising revenue too.
Rowena	It would be much better for the company if the financial balance were less erratic from one month to the next. Also I would like to look at how you are going to establish your budget for the new costing system.

Pierre	I've not really thought about the budget yet. I've been too taken up with the monthly variations. Can the budget wait?
Rowena	Well, if we looked at that next week, we could focus today on the variations.
Pierre	Yes, I would really like to deal with the variations, then perhaps I can turn my mind to the new system for our next session.

Notice how Rowena and Pierre worked together to establish the aims of this coaching session.

AWARENESS

In this phase of the coaching, your aim is to develop your pupil's awareness of the subject and issues. There may be some aspects of the subject of which the pupil is well aware, but others that are yet to emerge. As a coach, your task in this phase of the coaching is to develop your pupil's awareness.

The coach helps the pupil develop awareness of the issues.

The crucial point here is that the focus is pupil-centred. You are concerned with developing the pupil's awareness, not on showing your own grasp of the situation. Any information from you as coach needs to be very modest. Pupils may grab at such input and focus on it to the exclusion of their own ideas. It is a good discipline to practise focusing entirely on the pupil's perspective. When you are used to this and comfortable with this approach, you may then start to give some input yourself.

In this expanding phase the crucial skills are listening, reflecting and enquiring.

Rowena has some thoughts on the origin of Pierre's problems, but focuses on helping him identify the ones that he sees.

Rowena So, what are the issues then?

Pierre The production costs are increased by any increase in the number of pages, and this can vary for each issue. I don't have any direct control over that. Also the advertising revenue depends on the number of advertisements sold, and that is unpredictable.

Rowena You seem to have two different factors here.

Pierre Well, they are not completely separate. We may be planning to fill the usual number of pages, and then a late advert is placed, and this pushes up the page count. If it's only one advert, the extra revenue doesn't cover the extra costs and we run into deficit. If there were two, it would generate profit.

Rowena You must feel uncertain how the costs will balance each month.

Pierre Yes, it's not really under my control, yet I am responsible for the financial management.

Rowena has helped Pierre identify the factors in his problem, and he has named a crucial issue – he feels responsible without having control.

ANALYSIS

The coach helps the pupil analyse the issues and options for action.

Once the issues have been established, possible approaches to the problem can be analysed. In this phase of the coaching session the coach encourages the pupil to evaluate and analyse the issues that have been identified and the options for addressing them. Analysing the 'pros and cons' of an option may help the pupil eliminate some options as outside candidates.

In this phase of the session, the coach prompts the pupil

to enquire further into the issues, or the coach may make enquiries.

By the end of the analysis phase, the pupil should have clarified which options he or she wants to pursue.

Rowena	What would have to happen so that you could manage the balance for each issue better?
Pierre	Maybe I have to be consulted before there is a decision that increases the page count above the target.
Rowena	How would that help?
Pierre	I could redo the costing to see what the effect would be.
Rowena	And is there any downside to that?
Pierre	I doubt that it would be popular with Juliet. She likes to be able to respond directly if an advertiser phones up ... and I'm not always available at short notice for such decisions.
Rowena	What other options are there?
Pierre	I suppose we could cut some feature or editorial to keep the page count down, but Brian won't like that.
Rowena	What do you think the real problem is here, Pierre?
Pierre	Well basically there are conflicting interests between Juliet and Brian. We need to improve the coordination.
Rowena	You seem to have a clear understanding of the issues.

ACTION

In this phase of the coaching session the coach helps pupils identify how to implement the necessary actions they need to take to move things forward.

The predominant skills the coach uses at this stage are

The coach helps the pupil identify actions to be taken.

focusing and teaching. It is important that the action is clear and achievable. Here are some examples:

- Learn about . . .
- Experiment with and find out how . . .
- Clarify . . .
- Sort out . . .

It may be that you as coach are able to help pupils learn a skill. This may be very helpful, provided pupils want to be shown the skill. If you offer skills prematurely and before pupils have decided they want you to teach them, it can leave pupils feeling inadequate – that others know better.

Actions should include follow-up so that the effectiveness of the agreed actions can be checked.

Rowena So what actions do you propose?

Pierre Well, I can tell Juliet and Brian they've got to agree on the page count. I'm not sure they will listen to me. You may have to tell them.

Rowena sees that Pierre needs some instruction here on how to engender cooperation among the three of them.

Rowena Telling people they've got to do something usually creates resentment, and then they don't do it well anyway. How could you avoid having to tell them?

Pierre looks uncertain. Rowena spends some time teaching Pierre how to have an open discussion with Brian and Juliet about the problem. He then seems more ready to have a go himself.

Rowena So what actions have you settled on?

Pierre I am going to set up a meeting with Brian and Juliet at which I will discuss the problem of the cost balance, and how it is dependent on the actions they are taking. I will be looking for

> some arrangement so that we can coordinate the acceptance of new advertisements with adjustment of editorial or feature space.
>
> **Rowena** And how will you follow this action up?
>
> **Pierre** I'll report back to you at our next session, and confirm the arrangements at the team meeting next month.

ASSESSMENT

The final stage of the process is a chance for the coach and pupil to assess the learning and outcome. Completing the loop in this way helps pupils increase their pace of learning in the future. It is also an opportunity to affirm the pupils' work.

Assessing the session together improves future coaching sessions.

> **Rowena** OK, so, before we finish – how has this session been for you? What have you found useful?
>
> **Pierre** Well, I hadn't realized how the balancing problem sprang from the separate interests of Juliet and Brian.
>
> **Rowena** Anything else?
>
> **Pierre** Well, yes. I thought you would have to sort it out. Now I can see that if I tell them about the problem, we may be able to find a mutual arrangement – and that would be better than you having to lay down the law.
>
> **Rowena** I've appreciated how well you have assessed the situation, and how you are willing to develop a mutually acceptable approach between the three of you. I'm glad you will be doing this and I don't have to become involved! OK, let's leave it there.

WHAT ABOUT YOUR OWN VIEWS?

Coaches have their own views. What place do they have?

The primary objective in coaching is for pupils to identify for themselves the way forward. If they make the choices then they will have the motivation and commitment to see them through. You, as coach, may sometimes have views about which options or approaches are desirable or even unwise or impracticable. If you find yourself wanting a pupil to adopt a particular approach more than others, check out with yourself why this is.

Possible reasons for you as coach favouring some approaches above others could be:

- Your own experience showed one approach more satisfactory than another.
- You had a bad experience related to a proposed approach.
- You would like the pupil to benefit from your wisdom.
- You would like the pupil to avoid the pitfalls you have seen.
- You think it would be best if the pupil adopted your approach.
- You enjoy using your insight and wisdom.

Some of these reasons may be sound. Others may come from your need to 'have the answers' or to be helpful. Might these move the focus away from the pupil to the coach?

Having reflected on these factors, you may still feel it important to give some guidance or advice. There are at least two ways you can do this. You can focus the pupil on the issues that concern you, in the expectation that the pupil will then see the problem or pitfall that you anticipate.

Alternatively, you can simply state your position or preference. If you have a strong reason why you want the pupil to adopt one approach rather than another, it may be most straightforward to say so, owning it as your own. If this is what you want, do not spend time allowing pupils to develop their own options only to have you override them or manipulate them away to your preference. Consider a statement like: 'Perhaps it would be best to complete the alternative strategies report before evaluating the new system proposal.' This is vague. The pupil is left unsure why it would be best.

Alternatively, you might say: 'You have already identified that if you give priority to the new system proposal, this will delay the alternative strategies report by a week. I really do need that report in time for the management meeting on the 23rd. I need you to do that first.' Here the pupil is clear what you require, and why.

A NOTE ON TIME BOUNDARIES

Sometimes it may be tempting to extend a session beyond an agreed time. Consider this carefully before doing so. Not only may this disrupt other schedules and lead to the coaching sessions consuming too much time, but it can also detract from the pupil's responsibility to sort things out within the structures provided.

Sometimes pupils may raise new issues when there is insufficient time to deal with them. They may drop a 'bombshell' in the closing minutes of the session, or even on the way out of the room – the 'door-handle' aside. You will have to decide whether the issue is sufficiently important to extend the session. Remember that pupils may choose this moment precisely because there is limited time available. Perhaps they do not want to get into this subject in depth at that moment. Often it is best to respect this hesitancy, to acknowledge what has been said and to leave the way open for it to be discussed at a more appropriate time.

Maintaining boundaries is an important contribution to making the session safe.

As Pierre is leaving his session with Rowena he throws in:

Pierre   You know, we do have some real communication problems.

Rowena feels tantalized by this aside. Why is Pierre mentioning this on his way out of the room? Does he really want to get into this now? She decides Pierre should raise it at a more appropriate time if he wants to pursue it.

Rowena   I would be interested to hear your views on that – it sounds important. I suggest you raise it next time we meet.

IN SUMMARY

We have seen how the six phases of the coaching session give it the critical shape of expanding and then focusing. Figure 6.1 illustrates how these fit together.

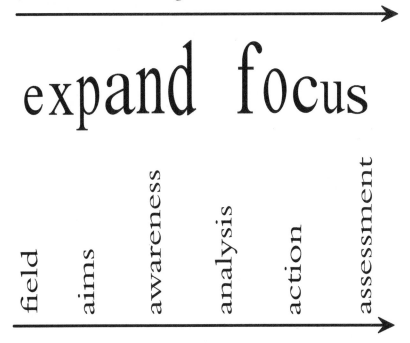

FIGURE 6.2: Coaching session shape and phases

ACTION LIST

1. Check that you understand the shape of a coaching session, how it expands the information available and then focuses it.
2. Study the six sub-phases, and revisit the examples of Rowena's sessions to see how she shaped her session with Pierre.
3. Reflect on how you use your own experience and views in a helping interaction.
4. List your alternative strategies in the situation of one of your people making a 'door-handle' aside. How might you choose to deal with it?

CHAPTER 7

STARTING TO COACH

Once begun, a task is easy; half the work is done.
Horace, *Epistles*, (8 BC)

KEY LEARNING POINTS

In this chapter you will be encouraged to start coaching yourself by:

- **experiencing coaching**
- **arranging practice sessions**
- **carrying out actual coaching sessions yourself**

INTRODUCTION

The time has come for you make a start in coaching or, if you already coach, to start actively using the skills and structure of superior coaching.

In this chapter we cover three ways of practising and getting experience, and also look at feedback – how to learn from experience.

RECEIVING COACHING

A central tenet of this book is that one of the best ways of learning a new skill is to be coached in it. If you can, arrange for you yourself to be coached in your coaching, by your manager or some other colleague.

Coaches benefit from being coached themselves.

This has four main advantages:

- You can use it to receive coaching in your planning and introduction of the coaching approach.
- As a receiver of coaching, you will get first-hand experience of what it is like, what is helpful and what is unhelpful.
- Your manager will be involved and gain better understanding of what you are setting out to achieve.
- You can let your people know that you yourself have coaching. It is not just something 'they' receive.

The best environment will be one in which you receive supportive coaching from someone who either practises superior coaching or is endeavouring to develop it.

Even if the coaching you receive is not what you would like, you may be able to learn from it. You may experience approaches or interventions that you would not want to use yourself for your pupils. Becoming aware of this is important learning, and your own coaching will benefit from it.

You can learn even from poor coaching.

I cannot emphasize enough the importance of having appropriate support in your endeavour. I often come across what I call 'competent manager' syndrome. This is the belief that managers need personally to shoulder responsibility as proof of their competency. Superior managers are not the ones who struggle on without support, carrying all the responsibility themselves. Superior managers are the ones who arrange their work and support so that they can do their job well without becoming overburdened, still be available to their people and still have a balanced life.

Superior managers are those who arrange good support for themselves.

If you are working in an environment in which you are unable to get this support from your management, consider making arrangements with someone from outside your organization. There are individuals and organizations who provide mentoring or coaching services on a professional basis.

PRACTICE SESSIONS

One very effective way to practise and gain confidence is to set up practice sessions with your people. Work in a group of three (or four if need be). Exercise 12 provides a structure for this.

Exercise 12 – Coaching in practice groups of three

1. Agree the time you have together. Divide it among you and then divide that into coaching time and feedback time. For example, if there are three of you and you have one hour overall, you have 20 minutes each. You could use this as 15 minutes coaching and 5 minutes feedback.
2. Identify yourselves as A, B and C.
3. A coaches B while being observed by C.
4. C then gives feedback to A on what C observed. Note that C should refrain from making coaching comments to B.
5. Roles are then rotated so that everybody has a turn. I suggest the following sequence:

Turn	Coach	Pupil	Observer
1	A	B	C
2	C	A	B
3	B	C	A

You can work in a group of four using two observers.
6. Before concluding, spend a few moments checking out how the structure worked for you and how you would like to improve it next time.

Table A3.2 in Appendix 3 provides a checklist for observers to help them give useful feedback.

COACHING FOR REAL

Some people are reluctant to launch themselves into a new activity. They may feel self-conscious, or nervous.

You may find it helpful to arrange your early sessions with a pupil with whom you feel at ease and with whom you can be open about your coaching work. If you become stuck, ask for some guidance from your pupil.

Corrie has been receiving coaching from Rowena and is now holding her first coaching session with her clerical assistant, Colin. She is feeling rather self-conscious about this, so she starts by explaining to Colin how the coaching will aim to support him in developing his skills. She says she may be asking for guidance from him at times, and will want some feedback. They agree on half an hour for their first session.

About halfway through Corrie begins to feel lost and uncertain how she is doing.

Corrie   I'm beginning to feel lost, and I'm not sure this is getting anywhere. Can we just hold it for a moment. How are you finding this?

Colin   Well, I've been enjoying it up until a few moments ago. I really like working with you on improving my work. But in the last minutes I began to feel we were going round in circles. We seem to have analysed this matter to death.

Corrie is encouraged by Colin's response and realizes she needs to move from 'analysis' into 'actions'.

In any superior coaching session there should be an opportunity for some assessment and feedback on the coaching process. For a coach learning new skills it may be helpful to give rather more attention to this than would be appropriate for an 'old hand'. The coach can ask for feedback from the pupil and can also assess the session from the coach's perspective. Use Tables A3.3 and A3.4 in Appendix 3 as guides for this.

ACTION LIST
1. Start coaching!
2. Set up some practice sessions with your colleagues, using the structure in Exercise 12.
3. Arrange to receive some coaching yourself.
4. Start coaching for real. Ask for feedback from your pupil(s) and use it to improve your skills.

PART 3

CORE SKILLS
IN DEPTH

This part of the book covers the core skills of coaching in more depth, and provides opportunity to practise and develop them.

KEY LEARNING POINTS

The following are the key learning points in the four chapters of Part Three:

■ how to be more effective in active listening
■ how to help pupils explore their issues, enquire into ways forward and focus on actions
■ how to teach pupils appropriately
■ how to give feedback and support
■ how to challenge and confront

By now you will have learnt the key aspects of coaching – the values, the core skills and the shape of a session – and you will have started to put them into practice. I introduced the core skills in outline, so that you could get a feel for them and start using them as soon as possible.

In this part of the book we shall return to the core skills of active listening, enquiring and teaching in more depth. You will have the opportunity to learn about them in more detail, and to practise them further.

We shall also develop the skill of affirming to include feedback and support, and introduce the counterpart – challenge.

I believe you will develop these skills best in parallel with your actual coaching practice, rather than attempting to develop them in isolation.

CHAPTER 8

ACTIVE LISTENING

Ear

You

Eyes

Undivided
Attention

Heart

FIGURE 8.1: To listen

KEY LEARNING POINTS

In this chapter you will have the opportunity to:

- learn about active listening in more depth, including attending, listening and reflecting
- learn about the use of silence
- extend your skills by using summarizing and linking
- develop your use of questions
- practise active listening skills

INTRODUCTION

Listening is perhaps the single most important skill for the coach. Before you can presume to coach people in developing the skills they need, you need to hear clearly what their needs are.

You may think that listening is something we do all the time; however much of the listening that goes on is not just about hearing what the other person needs. Frequently what we hear is subtly influenced by our own needs and what we would like to hear. Further, in most informal situations listening is a two-way process. In a balanced relationship there is a balance in the listening. I talk to my friend for a while then, perhaps, he talks about something of interest to him. We both get something out of it.

In social interactions listening is balanced between the needs of both parties.

Indeed in most social listening we pick up on what we hear and use it to develop our own interest.

> Pierre and Juliet are chatting in the coffee area.
>
> **Juliet** I've been dying for this coffee … it's been absolute chaos this morning since the system crashed. I lost all of this morning's work.
>
> **Pierre** Yeah … I'm behind on my summary report for the meeting after lunch. Mind you I do a 'save' regularly, so I only lost ten minutes of work.
>
> **Juliet** I suppose I should have done, but it's too late now.

In this short exchange Pierre responds with his experience of the incident, based on his own interest. His comment about how he saves his work regularly could be seen as helpful but could also be motivated by needing to let Juliet know he feels smarter than her. Whatever Pierre's motives, Juliet feels inferior and that her oversight is exposed. In a coaching situation this is unnecessary and counterproductive. Juliet learnt the wisdom of saving her work the minute she found she had lost it.

In this chapter, listening skills are introduced in more depth and you will have the opportunity to practise them yourself.

ATTENDING

The first step in really listening to someone is to start attending to them fully.

In an informal coaching conversation that has arisen spontaneously it may be difficult to attend fully. There may be other conversations going on, or other distracting activity. You may need to recognize the limitations of this situation and transfer the conversation to a more suitable venue.

If I allow other people to interrupt I am letting my pupil know that this session is less important than the other distractions. If we do not have privacy, then I am creating a situation in which my pupil will probably not feel safe enough to raise any difficult issues – perhaps the ones that are most crucial of all.

We need to attend fully if we are to listen well.

Coaches must largely suspend their own needs to focus on the needs of their pupils. If I cannot find this space, time or privacy, then it also says something about me. Perhaps I like to be seen to be busy and organize my working life accordingly, even unconsciously. Perhaps I need to have some coaching for myself on how I organize things!

In Chapter 5 I indicated that part of attending can be to face the other person, keep comfortable eye contact, avoid fidgeting, etc. While these can be important, real attention is something that cannot be faked. If I pretend to attend while my mind is on other things, then my 'attention' will not really be effective. Ways in which I may be able to improve the quality of my attention include:

- making sure I have somewhere else that I can deal with issues that might otherwise intrude here;
- learning to note the intrusion to myself and let it go for now;

- taking some brief action that attends to the intrusion so that I can release it.

LISTENING

In listening, coaches focus on hearing what their pupils have to say. They suspend their own needs including their need to have answers or insights. In its simplest form, listening involves responding with an attentive silence, which invites the speaker to continue and say more.

Listening is hearing what the other person is saying.

In practice it helps the listening process if speakers receive an acknowledgement of what they are saying that does not take the focus away from them. This acknowledgement of 'message received' is given almost unconsciously by most listeners, perhaps with subtle body language such as nods, or eye movements. When listening on the telephone we are obliged to use more audible acknowledgements. Listen to someone listening on the telephone, and you will hear things like: 'Mmm … oh … mmm … really? … ah … tut …'.

REFLECTING

When people talk to each other, they often repeat the same message in various forms. They need to know they have been heard and understood before they are free to move on to the next thought. The grunts and other non-verbal acknowledgements may confirm that the words have been heard but may not acknowledge that the meaning has been understood.

In active listening this acknowledgement process is taken further, by the listener reflecting back a short summary or paraphrase of what has been heard. To do this we have to concentrate on what is being said, absorb each 'paragraph', digest it and find a way of summarizing it in our words. Remember, we are not trying to 'add value' by slipping in our experience or opinions, nor are we inserting advice. We are simply reflecting back a short summary of what we have heard. However, it must be in our own words so that it is clear we are not simply repeating what has been heard without

In reflecting we acknowledge what we have heard.

perhaps having understood the meaning. There are three key effects of this process:

1. It disciplines listeners to focus on what speakers are saying, rather than on their own ideas and solutions.
2. It lets speakers know they have been heard, and thus frees them to move on to the next thought.
3. If listeners have not understood correctly what speakers wanted them to know, the speakers will automatically correct the misunderstanding.

Let us return to Juliet's morning. This time she is talking to her coach Rowena who uses active listening.

Juliet It's been absolute chaos this morning since that system hiccup. I lost all of this morning's work.
Rowena Oh?

Here Rowena is acknowledging what Juliet has said but is leaving an inviting space for more.

Juliet Yes, and I was already behind because of having to get the account statistics from branch offices because Paul's off sick.

Rowena now has a sense of Juliet's theme and reflects it back.

Rowena You really are busy at the moment, and losing your work this morning has made it worse.

Juliet feels heard, and is free to move on to her next thought, about her workload.

Juliet Yes, and I've got more of Paul's work to do.
Rowena So losing your work this morning has really put you in a difficult position.
Juliet It's not just about this morning. With Paul being away I've just got more than I can handle ... and it's a short week next week because of the bank holiday.

Rowena had misheard Juliet's emerging concern as being about her position at work. Juliet has corrected her by reinforcing her critical issue. Rowena reflects her corrected understanding.

Rowena   So it's not just today that's worrying you but the overload you anticipate next week as well.

Rowena has now correctly acknowledged the emerging theme of Juliet's workload, and Juliet is free to move on.

Juliet   I really don't know how I am going to manage next week.

Juliet arrives at a major statement of her concern.

Notice how Rowena refrained from offering wisdom or solutions, but concentrated on hearing what Juliet had to say. Even though she misheard Juliet's underlying concern at one point, Juliet corrected her. Her acknowledgement of the compounding pressure led on to Juliet identifying her anticipated problems of next week.

At this stage in the coaching Rowena is not concerned with offering solutions. Had she done so, for example by telling Juliet to save her work more regularly, the impending problem next week might not have emerged.

USE OF SILENCE

The right word may be effective, but no word was ever as effective as a rightly timed pause.
Mark Twain, *Speeches*, ed A.B. Paine (1923)

You talk when you cease to be at ease with your thoughts.
Kahlil Gibran, *The Prophet* (1926)

Our world and certainly many business environments are

filled with the sound of activity. If we are busy, we assume something must be happening. Actually, it is not always like that. Perhaps in our culture we miss the stillness within which a new awareness can emerge, or a creative idea can first crystallize.

A vital aspect of coaching is to create a space in which pupil and coach can reflect, and in which new thoughts or ideas can emerge. This takes time.

Leaving space is perhaps somewhat alien in our culture. Perhaps we feel we 'ought' to have something to say. If we say nothing for a while, we may fear we shall be seen to have no answer or nothing to contribute when we feel we should have. When we speak for such reasons, it is to make ourselves more comfortable and we are thus moving away from the pupil's needs. We are also depriving our pupil of one of the most powerful and helpful of all interventions – silence. This is not to say that silence is always helpful. It can also be used ominously and threateningly.

Leaving silence is a powerful intervention.

What is important is that I, as a coach, can leave silence when it may be helpful, or when I have nothing in particular to say. If I need to break a silence because I am uncomfortable rather than because I have something useful to say, then at least I should be aware of what I am doing.

For pupils a silence may be a welcome relief from the need to respond, or a chance to reflect a while. Some may find silence uncomfortable. It is a matter of fine judgement for coaches to decide whether to break the silence to ease the stress on the pupil, or whether to leave the space open to see what happens. When pupils are feeling uncomfortable with a silence and need to break it, they may say something spontaneous and possibly unguarded. This can be helpful in identifying issues that might otherwise be held back as inappropriate or unacceptable. However, coaches should treat such impromptu utterances respectfully rather than use them against the speaker.

Rowena continues listening to Juliet.

Juliet   I really don't know how I am going to manage next week.

Rowena You feel under a lot of pressure to cope.

There is a pause while they reflect on this situation. Rowena refrains from filling the space, perhaps by trying to reassure Juliet, or telling her how she can cope.

Juliet   When work piles up I feel pressured … and then I can't cope.

There is a further pause of some 20 seconds while Juliet reflects on what she has just said.

Juliet   I feel inadequate when I can't cope. You must think I'm awful.

The space that Rowena left has created the opportunity for Juliet to develop a further and more personal theme. In particular she has, for the first time, named her fear about what Rowena thinks of her.

A WORD ON EXERCISES AND FEEDBACK SKILLS

At several points in this book there are exercises in which one person, whom we shall call 'A', practises the skills of a coach, while another 'B' takes the role of pupil. 'B' will then give feedback to 'A'.

Feedback skills are covered in Chapter 11. However, at this stage, it will be helpful if I introduce the basics you will need to give effective feedback in these exercises. The purpose of feedback is to let 'A' know what 'B' experienced. For example, 'B' might say 'I don't think you heard how important that aspect was for me'. 'A' should avoid responding in self-justification or disagreement, perhaps, by saying something like 'Oh, but I did hear that'. The crucial

Giving and receiving feedback effectively are themselves skills.

point is that 'B' did not feel heard. Feedback is often most effective when 'A' hears the feedback in silence and accepts whatever is helpful to them, and lets go of anything unhelpful. 'B', in giving feedback, needs to respect the process and not use it to put in anything to which 'A' might feel a need to respond, such as a 'dig'. If there is any discussion it should focus on how 'A' might have been more effective. *Avoid getting into the content of what was discussed.*

LISTENING PRACTICE

It is by practising that we learn new skills. The structured and disciplined listening introduced in this chapter is a new skill, and it needs practising.

When I first learnt active listening, I found I had to concentrate hard. At first I felt awkward – a bit like wobbling when I had just learnt to ride a bicycle. I also felt self-conscious, and that others must think I sounded odd and clumsy. Further, I was not using my established ways of listening, and I felt 'de-skilled' for some time. At first I had to concentrate hard and 'switch in' to listening mode. Now, years later, I have integrated careful listening. It comes quite naturally, and I feel relaxed about it.

You will need to practise listening. You could do this as part of your coaching sessions, but I recommend that you arrange listening practice among your people or with a colleague, using the structured exercises that follow. These exercises allow you to focus on a particular aspect of listening. Taking turns with each other is not only an equitable arrangement but it is helpful, when developing your listening skills, to experience being listened to.

Exercise 13 – Listening practice

1. Make arrangements to practise listening in a pair using acknowledgements, silence and reflecting.
2. Meet together in privacy for an agreed period, and divide the time up, for example:
   - A listens to B   5 minutes
   - B gives feedback to A   2 minutes
   - B listens to A   5 minutes
   - A gives feedback to B   2 minutes
3. Repeat the sequence so you have a chance to improve through what you have learnt.

Total time planned (allowing swap-over time)   30 minutes

In the first stage, 'B', the person being listened to, can choose to talk about any subject at all. It might be an issue at work but it could also be about an issue at home, or an interest such as his or her golf swing. 'A', the listener, focuses on listening as described, initially using acknowledgements, silences and reflecting.

When the listening has finished, 'B' gives feedback to 'A'. The purpose of feedback is to let 'A' know how well 'B' felt heard. I have provided a checklist in Table 8.1.

TABLE 8.1: Checklist for feedback on listening

1. How well did I feel heard?
2. What helped me to feel heard?
3. What made me feel less well heard?
4. What did the listener do or say that I appreciated?
5. What did the listener do or say that I did not like or found unhelpful?
6. Is there anything that I would have liked to have talked about that remained unsaid? If so, how might the listener have created the space in which I might have done so?

Listening very attentively as propounded here needs practice, and you will probably need to practise it more than once.

SUMMARIZING

During active listening the coach has been listening carefully and reflecting back whenever a 'paragraph' of thoughts has been presented, attaching a theme to that paragraph. As this continues, the number of separate 'paragraphs of thoughts' builds up. Skilled coaches will occasionally reflect back not just the latest paragraph, but a short summary of the recent paragraphs. They collect them into a 'chapter' and give them an abstract summary. This helps both coaches and pupils to keep track of the thoughts as they develop; moreover it frees pupils to develop their thinking further.

In summarizing we collect paragraphs of thoughts, and label a chapter.

Rowena decides to summarize.

Rowena Losing your work this morning has increased the pressure you feel, and you don't know how you will manage next week. You fear you can't cope under pressure, and then you feel inadequate.
Juliet   Yes ... that's true.

Now Juliet can begin to see a picture of how she got into this situation.

LINKING

Sometimes coaches may notice similarities with other themes from earlier on in the session or from previous sessions. Coaches can, at this point, draw attention to the link. This can be seen as noting a cross-reference.

We can make links to draw out common themes.

Linking can be particularly powerful in helping pupils identify emerging themes.

Rowena recalls that this is not the first time Juliet has had this difficulty and links it to previous events.

Rowena I recall you had difficulty coping a couple of months ago when you were under pressure while the Edinburgh branch was being established, and before that when the new accounting system was being introduced.

This linking helps Juliet see that today's incident is not just an isolated one, but a part of a general theme for her: that when she comes under pressure, she finds it difficult to cope.

FURTHER PRACTICE

Once you as listener feel comfortable with the practice of the basic listening skills of acknowledgements, silences and reflecting, as described earlier in this chapter, you can start to introduce summarizing and linking. You may need more time for this, and an extended time schedule is provided in Exercise 14. For feedback use the checklist in Table 8.1.

Exercise 14 – Extending listening skills

1. Make an arrangements with your people or a colleague to practise listening to each other in pairs using acknowledgements, silence and reflecting, and also summarizing and linking. You may need to allow more time.
2. Meet together in privacy for an agreed period, and divide the time up, for example:
   - A listens to B   7 minutes
   - B gives feedback to A   2 minutes
   - B listens to A   7 minutes
   - A gives feedback to B   2 minutes
3. Repeat the sequence so you have a chance to improve through what you have learnt.

Total time planned (allowing for swap-over time)   40 minutes

THE ROLE OF QUESTIONS

You may have noticed how few questions there have been in the example dialogues. Let us consider the issue of questions.

At its simplest level we might assume that a question is asked because the questioner wants to know the answer. However, frequently questioners have some other less obvious motive. Consider for example the question time at the end of a presentation or lecture. Questions are often asked with the purpose, at least in part, of displaying the understanding or knowledge of the questioner, or displaying superior knowledge to the person being questioned. Neither of these is simply because the questioner wants to know the answer. If you doubt this, check whether you have ever felt a need to get your question in before someone else asks it, or felt disappointed if someone else asks your question. If you were only interested in the answer, you would feel satisfied or even pleased if someone else asked the question and thus saved you the trouble of doing so.

Many questions are not put just to get an answer.

Similarly questions put by a coach can have hidden agendas, such as showing off the coach's knowledge, or showing up the pupil.

It is a good exercise to try replacing a question with the honest statement that you could use instead, and see what emerges. Here are a few examples:

Question: Didn't you think to save your work in case the system went down?

Statement: I think you should have saved your work regularly.

Question: When did you first realize that the contractor was going to be late?

Statement: You should have spotted this earlier.

Question: Do you realize how much overall delay this is going to cause?

Statement: I feel you have let me down and you are in trouble.

Sometimes the agenda for a question is carried not so much through the words as by emphasis or non-verbal signals.

Consider the question: 'How much delay will there be in completing the test phase?' You might suppose that the questioner needs to know how much delay there will be. However, even subtle stress in a sentence can change its impact significantly. Try repeating this question aloud with the stress on different words, and listen for the statement behind the emphasis. Table 8.2 gives some examples.

TABLE 8.2: Examples of how stress carries implication

SENTENCE STRESS	POSSIBLE IMPLICATION
'*How much* delay will there be in completing the test phase?'	I don't believe you know how much.
'How much *delay* will there be in completing the test phase?'	This delay is really screwing things up.
'How much delay *will* there be in completing the test phase?'	I don't think you've been honest with me.
'How much delay will there be in *completing* the test phase?'	I think you underestimate the time to do the whole job properly.

If you do have an opinion or view, you have a choice whether to give it or not. You may choose to withhold it for a while so that your pupil can find something important for themselves, or you may decide to make it known. If you have an opinion to give, it is better to give it as such, rather than to put it indirectly as a question. Giving your own views will be covered in Chapter 11.

There are two dimensions of every question for the coach to consider:

1. How does the question help the pupil?
2. What does the question achieve for the coach?

In Table 8.3 I offer four broad classifications for a question.

TABLE 8.3: Classifying question motives

TYPE	EXAMPLE MOTIVE
Clarifying	I did not understand something. Please clarify.
Prowess	Look what a clever person I am.
Controlling or punitive	You are in trouble.
Exploring	I want to help you explore this aspect more.

Try expressing the question 'How much delay will there be in completing the test phase?' in a way that fits each of these classifications.

Consider for yourself which styles of question superior coaches use and which they avoid.

ACTION LIST

1. Form a partnership in which you can practise your listening skills.
2. Study the basic components of active listening (listening, reflecting and silence) and note how Rowena uses them.
3. Practise these basic skills with your partner by using Exercise 13 repeatedly until you feel comfortable with it.
4. Then study how to extend your active listening by including summaries and linking.
5. Practise active listening including summaries and linking.
6. Use your developing active listening skills in your actual coaching sessions.
7. Become aware of how you use any questions in your listening.

CHAPTER 9

EXPLORING, ENQUIRING AND FOCUSING

One doesn't discover new lands without consenting to lose sight of the shore for a very long time.

André Gide, *The Counterfeiters*, 3.15 (1925)

KEY LEARNING POINTS

In this chapter you will have the opportunity to learn more about:

- helping pupils explore their options, enquire into issues and focus on action
- styles of questions
- the use of silence in exploring
- mixing these interventions

INTRODUCTION

A crucial part of coaching is the expanding of pupils' awareness of the situation and pupils' options. Particularly during this phase of the session, but also at other times, you will be exploring with your pupils. In this chapter we cover in more depth the skills that help pupils explore further.

I see the role of the coach in exploration as a guide engaged to accompany an explorer. In some instances the explorer may be venturing through territory well known to the guide. In such cases the guide may take a role of leading. However, if he or she simply leads, the explorer will gain little, apart from getting from A to B. A good guide is able to help the explorer discover the territory for him or herself. The explorer comes with fresh eyes, and takes delight in things taken for granted by the guide. The guide, in turn, is able to learn much from these new insights and discoveries of the new explorer. The primary role of the coach is not to get pupils from A to B but to help pupils gain the skills with which they can get from A to B themselves and, moreover, from N to M and Y to Z.

The coach is like a guide for an explorer.

Sometimes the path is known to neither. However, the guide may be familiar with this sort of terrain and knows the sorts of hazard that may be met, how to gain sustenance, how to read the weather and how to avoid trouble. So, even though the guide does not know this particular territory intimately, he or she knows this type of territory in general.

The best guides are the ones who know how to find their way even when they become lost. Beware of guides who have never become lost, because they may be unskilled in finding their way again.

CLOSED AND OPEN QUESTIONS

Questions are one of the key ways in which the coach can help the pupil explore issues. However, questioning in a truly explorative way needs care and skill.

A question can have many purposes.

I have already pointed out in Chapter 8 (page 85) that you can use questions for a variety of purposes, many of which may not be compatible with the values of coaching. The way in which you phrase a question can be very significant in how useful it is to the pupil.

Consider the question: 'Did you realize there was going to be a problem with the financial forecast?' This is an example of a closed question, one that invites a factual answer, in this case 'yes' or 'no'. Once the pupil has answered, the coach will then have to find another intervention to move things on again. Further, this particular question could have inquisitorial overtones, perhaps inferring that the pupil should have realized there was going to be a problem.

An alternative, more open question might have been: 'What sort of problems did you anticipate with the financial forecast?' Here the pupil is being invited to explore and expand their thinking on the subject, and the question is not inquisitorial.

Open questions invite expansion and exploration.

Closed questions have an important role when clarifying or establishing necessary facts. However, when encouraging someone to explore, it is helpful to use mainly 'open' questions, to expand thinking or understanding. Many people who have not considered this matter tend to use closed questions out of habit.

Closed questions have a role in clarifying and narrowing.

Exercise 15 will help you and your people develop an open question style.

Exercise 15 – Developing an open question style

Set up a practice session using a 'three' as in Exercise 12. For each 'turn':

1. The person taking the role of pupil nominates a topic of their choice that they wish to explore.
2. The coach then has five minutes in which to help the pupil explore the topic, using open questions.
3. The observer keeps a score for the number of open and closed questions.

The roles are then rotated so that everybody has a turn to practise this. You can also do this exercise in a pair, using a tape-recorder. The pair can then score the questions together.

EXPLORING STATEMENTS

A further development of open questions is to use exploring statements. These are statements that invite the pupil to explore the subject without any pressure to answer a question. Developing our earlier example, the coach might say: 'There are many ways in which a financial forecast can come adrift.'

This is inviting the pupil to think along the lines of what problems may arise, without any expectation that the pupil responds at this time. This can create more space for reflection than even an open question.

SILENCE

In Chapter 8 we saw that silence can be a powerful intervention in developing the pupil's thinking. Skilfully used, silence can also be useful in helping a pupil explore a subject. Silence from the coach can be an invitation to think further and not to stop here. The skill, which you may need to develop, is to know just how much silence to use to facilitate exploration without it becoming oppressive or manipulative.

ROWENA HELPS JULIET EXPLORE

Earlier we followed Rowena listening to Juliet as she developed the theme of how she does not cope when under pressure. Now Rowena is helping Juliet explore her options. She uses a mix of open questions, exploring statements and silence.

Rowena	So when you come under pressure you feel you cannot cope. What options do you have that would help you to cope while Paul is away?
Juliet	I don't seem to have many. I could try to work faster, or maybe stay for the evenings.
Rowena	Mmm ... I wonder what other options there might be.

There is a period of reflection.

Juliet   I could try and get a 'temp' in.

Rowena   And how would that help?

Juliet   I think it might cause me more pressure. I would be very worried about a temp contacting customers, and it might give a poor impression. I think I would end up watching the temp as well as doing my own work.

Rowena   So that's one possibility. Perhaps there are others too.

Juliet   Maybe I could get help from some other member of staff.

Rowena leaves space for Juliet to reflect on this possibility.

Juliet   They would need to know the work a bit ... someone like Robert or Freddy.

PRACTISING A MIX OF EXPLORING INTERVENTIONS

Exercise 16 – Mixing exploring interventions

Set up a practice session using a 'three' as in Exercise 12. For each 'turn':

1. The person taking the role of pupil nominates a topic of their choice that they wish to explore.
2. The coach then has 10 minutes in which to help the pupil explore the topic, using a mix of open questions, exploring statements and silences.
3. The observer keeps a record of each type of intervention used and notes those that are particularly helpful or unhelpful.

The roles are then rotated so that everybody has a turn to practise this. You can also do this exercise in a pair, using a tape-recorder. The pair can then score the questions together.

ACTION LIST

1. Form a 'three' in which you can develop your exploring, enquiring and focusing skills. If you wish to continue in a pair, you will need a tape-recorder.
2. Learn the difference between open and closed questions, and then use Exercise 15 to discover your own question style.
3. Practise a mix of exploring interventions, using open questions, exploring statements and silence. Use the structure in Exercise 16.
4. Start to introduce these skills into your actual coaching sessions.

CHAPTER 10

*T*EACHING

He who wishes to teach us a truth should not tell it to us, but simply suggest it with a brief gesture, a gesture which starts an ideal trajectory in the air along which we glide until we find ourselves at the feet of the new truth.

Ortega Y Gasset, *Meditations on Quixote* (1914)

KEY LEARNING POINTS

In this chapter you will have the opportunity to:

■ learn about the role of teaching in coaching
■ learn about teaching knowlege and skills
■ practise teaching these as part of coaching
■ discover how your teaching matches pupil needs

INTRODUCTION

Perhaps before starting to read this book you may have considered coaching to be almost synonymous with teaching, and you may have noticed teaching has had relatively little attention. Coaching and teaching are not synonymous. Coaching is much broader than teaching, but includes teaching as one of its many facets.

Teaching within management coaching is not usually the

dominant activity. Rather it is used specifically when the pupil needs new information that the coach can give, or the pupil needs to acquire a new skill that can be most effectively learnt through demonstration by the coach. In both cases teaching is carried out because of the needs of the pupil.

In this chapter we look at the sort of teaching that is appropriate, and you will have the opportunity to practise your teaching skills.

APPROPRIATE TEACHING

Appropriate teaching has an important role in coaching.

It is important that coaches use teaching with their pupils when it is appropriate and in ways that are appropriate, and that coaches avoid inappropriate teaching. Use Exercise 17 for yourself and your people to develop an understanding about this.

Exercise 17 – Use of teaching in coaching

Arrange a discussion with your people on the use of teaching in coaching. Include in your deliberations:

1. What sort of teaching is appropriate in coaching?
2. What aspects of teaching might it be important to avoid in coaching?
3. How might you as coaches use teaching and still retain a pupil-centred focus?
4. What is it important for you personally to remember when teaching as a coach?

IMPARTING KNOWLEDGE

One important use of teaching is for the coach to impart knowledge to the pupil. Exercise 18 can help people develop skills in imparting knowledge effectively.

Exercise 18 – Practise imparting knowledge

1. Make an arrangement with a colleague to practise teaching by imparting knowledge.
2. Meet together for an agreed period, and divide the time up, e.g.:

   – A teaches B   10 minutes
   – B gives feedback to A   5 minutes
   – B teaches A   10 minutes
   – A gives feedback to B   5 minutes

   Total time planned   30 minutes
3. At the start of each session the pupil identifies a subject about which he or she would like to know more, and which the coach might be able to teach.
4. The coach then has the allotted time to teach the pupil something about this subject.
5. When giving feedback, the pupil should remember to focus on the pupil's experience of the session and avoid continuing a discussion of the subject being taught. (The discussion can always be continued later after the exercise has been completed.)
6. For feedback use the following checklist:
   – How much of the session was on the subject you wanted?
   – How was the pace – too fast, too slow, about right?
   – What extraneous information was there?
   – Are you aware of any areas you would have preferred to have learnt about that were omitted?
   – Did you feel empowered or disempowered by the session?
   – With hindsight, how would you, the pupil, want to have been taught differently?
   – What did you appreciate about the teaching?

TEACHING A SKILL

Another important use of teaching in coaching is when the coach teaches the pupil a skill, such as carrying out a procedure, using a computer, interacting effectively with people etc.

You can practise teaching a skill using Exercise 19.

Exercise 19 – Practise teaching a skill

1. Make an arrangement with a colleague to practise teaching someone skills.
2. Meet together for an agreed period, and divide the time up, e.g.:

– A teaches B	10 minutes
– B gives feedback to A	5 minutes
– B teaches A	10 minutes
– A gives feedback to B	5 minutes
Total time planned	30 minutes

3. At the start of each session the pupil identifies a skill that he or she would like to learn, and that the coach might be able to teach. Choose something that can reasonably be covered in the allotted time.
4. The coach then has the allotted time to teach the pupil the skill.
5. When giving feedback, the pupil should remember to focus on the pupil's experience of the session and avoid continuing the skill lesson. (The skill lesson can always be continued later after the exercise has been completed.)
6. For feedback use the following checklist:
   - Were you taught the skill you wanted to learn?
   - How was the pace – too fast, too slow, about right?
   - How well was the teaching focused on what you wanted to learn?
   - Are you aware of any aspects that you might have been taught but that were omitted?
   - Did you feel empowered to use this skill or disempowered by the coach's display of the skill?
   - With hindsight, what would you like to be different about the way you were taught?
   - What did you appreciate about the way you were taught?

ROWENA TEACHES JULIET SOME PLANNING

Earlier we followed Rowena coaching Juliet on how to manage the pressures of work.

Juliet has decided to look at getting some help with her workload over the coming week while Paul is away. Rowena sees that Juliet is now more aware of how she feels unable to cope when under pressure, and what she can do about next week. Rowena thinks Juliet could benefit from managing her time better.

Rowena So, you now have some actions you will take to cope with your workload next week. I note that your present overload crept up on you. How do you plan your workload?

Juliet Plan it?

Rowena Yes ... so that you can see in advance how much you have to do and when you will be able to do it. Also you can foresee when you will have more than you can handle without help.

Juliet I don't see how I could plan handling the advertising ... Either there is too much work or there isn't.

Rowena Possibly, but you might be able to plan, especially in the run-up to going to press.

Juliet I don't see how that can be done.

Rowena Would you like to go through the steps with me, of how you might do that?

Juliet Mmm ... yes that would be interesting ... but I'm not sure it would work for my work.

Rowena notes Juliet's concern that planning cannot help her work, so decided that she needs to teach Juliet in the context of Juliet's work.

Rowena The first step is to identify everything that has to be done. Write a list now on the whiteboard!

Juliet writes down a list of the things she does in her job.

Rowena Any more?

Juliet I can't think of any others at the moment.

Rowena OK. Now write against each one how much time it takes.

Juliet Well, for 'Sending out issues to advertisers' that's easy, but 'Processing advert orders' is more complicated. I can't say how long that takes – there are several parts to that.

Rowena OK, so break that down into sub-tasks.

Rowena takes Juliet through the stages of planning – work breakdown, estimation, dependencies and time allocation, etc.

Juliet Well, I can see how this works – it's neat. But I'm not too sure how it will work out in practice. Perhaps I need to go away and have a go myself. It might be helpful if I could go through a plan with you after that.

ACTION LIST

1. Arrange a discussion with your group on the role of teaching in coaching. Use Exercise 17.
2. In your pair, practise imparting knowledge using Exercise 18.
3. Still in your pair, use Exercise 19 to practise teaching a skill.
4. Start to incorporate teaching into your coaching practice when appropriate. Check how your pupil(s) experience your teaching.

CHAPTER 11

*F*EEDBACK, SUPPORT AND CHALLENGE

Criticism should not be querulous and wasting, all knife and root puller, but guiding, instructive, inspiring, a south wind, not an east wind.

Emerson, *Journals* (1947)

KEY LEARNING POINTS

In this chapter you will have the opportunity to learn:

- about the importance of feedback and support
- about positive and negative reactions
- about objectivity and subjectivity
- how and when to challenge
- how to practise these skills

INTRODUCTION

In the coaching process, coaches support their pupils in

improving their performance. Pupils will naturally want to have feedback on how they are doing. This is the process through which they gain support and encouragement, and discover what they need to work at further.

Pupils will be looking for feedback from a variety of sources, including those with whom they have informal contact as they apply their new skills in their work. While this is important, the feedback they get there may be complicated by other factors and will not necessarily be fair or disciplined.

The coaching relationship is an important one in which feedback can be given by someone who takes the feedback process seriously and who is skilled and disciplined in feedback skills.

You have already had opportunity to give feedback as part of the exercises in this book, and may have studied the brief guidance in Appendix 3. In this chapter we explore feedback in more detail, and you will have the opportunity to develop your skills in giving feedback to pupils and others.

IMPORTANCE OF FEEDBACK

We need feedback to improve our performance.

Most people need feedback in some way. It is the process through which we learn how we are doing, when we are making progress and to what we still need to attend. Without feedback we do not know whether our attempts to improve or master a situation are having success. Of course we often have our own ideas on this, but these can be wrong. We may believe we are making progress when others feel we are not, or we may be unable to see progress that others can see. Feedback is the opportunity to learn how others see us.

RECEIVING FEEDBACK

When hearing feedback, receivers are often tempted into debate or discussion, such as 'Yes, I know, but ...'. Such discussion takes away from what is being offered. I recommend that when receiving feedback you listen to what is being said and take space to reflect upon it. Sometimes the urge to respond comes from a need not to be seen to accept what may be difficult. By simply listening to what is being offered, you can accept what seems appropriate and release what does not fit.

Givers of feedback should recognize that the receiver should not need to respond, and they should therefore avoid giving feedback that may be unfair or to which the receiver is bound to want to respond.

The coaching relationship is one in which feedback can be given and received in a spirit of mutual trust and respect.

POSITIVE AND NEGATIVE RECEPTION

I once witnessed an occasion in which seventeen people gave feedback to one individual. Sixteen of them were very warm and supportive, while one was rather uninterested. The receiver of this feedback completely ignored the sixteen who had been positive and focused entirely on the one whose feedback had not been so welcome. This well illustrates how selective we can be in hearing feedback. You might suppose that such selection would work in favour of hearing just the good news, but many people are more skilled at hearing negative views of themselves.

There will, of course, also be those who only seem to hear the good news about themselves. This might be because they have an unreasonably rosy view of themselves, but in my experience selectiveness in hearing only positive news often masks a fear of criticism.

Fully hearing affirmation and confirmation of ourselves, without selective filtering or distortion, is surprisingly difficult for many people. However, to do so can be a very powerful experience.

Superior coaches will not just give skilled feedback but will monitor how that feedback is being received. Although, as I have stressed earlier, pupils are free to accept or reject feedback, coaches need to note when pupils mishear or are repeatedly selective about what they hear. They may need to draw attention to this.

It is not always as simple as whether something is positive or negative.

While pupils may see feedback as positive or negative, it is not always as simple as that. Inappropriately warm affirmation might delude the pupil and therefore be negative. Receiving difficult and challenging feedback, however unwelcome initially, can be an important event leading to positive change, and cannot always be labelled negative. What is important is that there is a balance of support and challenge over time.

OBJECTIVE AND SUBJECTIVE FEEDBACK

It is often stressed that feedback should be objective and hence presumably unbiased. In objective feedback, the feedback giver tries to avoid giving personal views and opinions, and instead reports factual information. He or she might, for example, say, 'I see the report you produced this month was on time and conformed to the company format'.

The importance of objectivity is often stressed – but subjectivity is a rich source of wisdom.

I am not convinced that it is possible or desirable to keep out personal reactions to someone. These views will communicate themselves in some way or other and, in any event, they are an important part of building a meaningful relationship.

I believe it is important that personal and subjective views are also communicated and that they are owned as such. To say 'Your report was not good enough' leaves the receiver judged and unclear in what way they have failed. On the other hand, 'I would have liked your report to have had a clearer analysis of the source of the problem' makes it clear that this is the speaker's opinion, and moreover it pinpoints what the speaker would have liked to have been different.

AFFIRMATION

We may need to learn to affirm our pupils.

An important part of feedback is to affirm pupils in their attempts to improve their performance. Both coach and pupils can take pleasure in pupils' progress. While this may seem obvious, it is not always a natural and satisfactory process. We have already seen that some pupils may have difficulty hearing affirmation. Coaches may have difficulty giving it or be parsimonious with it, perhaps because they are unused to receiving it themselves. Others may be inappropriately effusive, perhaps from a desire to be well liked.

Good affirmation is regular, to the point, and supportive. Feedback should be honest. Sometimes a coach may sense it would be helpful to encourage the pupil and yet finds it difficult to affirm their progress at this time. It would be inappropriate to invent something that contradicts reality. It can be very helpful to affirm instead the efforts that the pupil is making, if this is the case. An example might be: 'I can see your disappointment that you did not get the order as you hoped, but I can also see how hard you are working to improve your skills in closing a sale. I appreciate the effort you are putting into this.'

CHALLENGING SKILLS

I have introduced the core skills in the order in which I believe it is helpful to learn them; this is also the order in which you can start to introduce them into coaching sessions. I have left challenging until now.

Challenging can take many forms. Sometimes it is a small point, or a remark that leads pupils to reflect on difficulties. Sometimes there may come a time when a major challenge is appropriate. Pupils may need to be invited to face a difficulty or 'grasp the nettle'. Perhaps they are failing to make the necessary improvements so far, or are deluding themselves that they are making more progress than they actually are. Perhaps they are not seeing a problem that the coach can see. While much of the approach advocated in this book is in helping pupils to find their own way of managing problems and improving their performance, challenging also has an important role. Sometimes it can be the spur needed for pupils to really tackle a problem, or even to face lack of progress. Sometimes it can come as a relief – pupils may have been

Pupils may need to be challenged.

aware of a difficulty but unable to name it and address it. Once the coach has done so, coach and pupil can address the difficulty together.

There is a view that challenging is inappropriate in the early stages of a helping relationship. Some hold that it is necessary first to develop sufficient trust that the relationship can withstand challenges without alienation (Egan, 1986).

However, this order is not sacrosanct and, once you are comfortable with challenging skills, you may want to experiment by being more flexible about which interventions you use and when. It is not always necessary or desirable to keep, say, all challenges until the end. However, you need to judge how well the coaching relationship is developing, and at what stage it can stand the more challenging interventions. To be challenging, for example, at the beginning of an early session will probably put a pupil on the defensive – a position from which it may take a long time to recover, if ever.

I think the ability of pupils to handle challenges constructively varies tremendously from one pupil to another. With some pupils, challenges seem helpful quite early on, even in the first session. With others it may take a substantial period of work before they are ready to receive challenges constructively. The skill is to judge when challenging will be useful, and the level of challenge that will support the pupil's progress rather than impede it. When making a challenge it should be:

> It requires skill to challenge in a way that is constructive for the pupil.

1. *Direct* Avoid hints or allusions. These can leave the pupil wondering or speculating; it is better to say what you have to say rather than leave the pupil wondering what you are driving at. Give the challenge in person rather than through the written word, even if you have to follow it up in writing.
2. *Concise* Say what you have to say but make it as concise as possible. Avoid beating about the bush.

Remember that a challenge is made to help the pupil face a difficulty. It is important that it be constructive, rather than destructive. Sometimes we may harbour negative feelings or resentments. These can come flooding out in a challenge. It is important not to let things build up and appear all at once, but rather to deliver one or perhaps two points at a time.

It is important that feedback is balanced, and this is particularly so when giving challenges. If there are several points being made, it can be helpful to intermix 'positive' and 'negative' ones. Some people advocate sandwiching 'negative' feedback between positive points.

I want to be cautious about the concept of positive and negative feedback. Inappropriately warm or comforting feedback can be destructive and hence negative, and difficult challenges can often turn out to be positive experiences.

There may be times when a coach needs to make a major challenge, perhaps to help the pupil confront a serious problem or shortcoming. Certainly it may be beneficial to give some supportive feedback first. It is also important not to distract from the given challenge by rushing in with distracting reassurance. The pupil may need time to absorb and reflect on a major challenge. It may be a disservice to rescue the pupil from the heart-searching that is required to deal with a major challenge. What may be more appropriate here is to follow the challenge with support – such as confirmation that the coach is willing to work with the pupil in dealing with the particular problem.

Pupils may need time to absorb a challenge...

... and benefit from support rather than rescuing.

ROWENA CHALLENGES JULIET

Rowena has helped Juliet start planning her work better. Rowena anticipated that Juliet would return to their next session with some sort of plan to manage her work. Juliet has not drafted a plan, but is throwing all her energy into coping with the pressure of work.

Rowena At our last session you learnt how to plan your work.

Juliet Yes, but I just haven't had time to do any more

	on that. The pressure has mounted and I don't know how I can manage to do the urgent things. Also I've had to revise the Midland's circulation list for Corrie – that took an extra day.
Rowena	I appreciate how helpful you have been to Corrie, and I note that it's to you that Corrie turns when she needs help. But I also see you with more work than you can handle, and now you're feeling unable to cope. It seems to me that you have taken on more tasks than you can manage – and then feel swamped by it all.
Juliet	Well, Corrie needed help.

Juliet does not seem to have accepted her own part in overloading herself, and Rowena decides to confront this.

Rowena   You are very supportive of others. Sometimes that's nice, but I do see you overloading yourself and then unable to cope – and that's not good for you or the department. You become overloaded because you take on more than you can manage. I think you *must* learn how to manage your commitments.

There is a pause while Juliet absorbs this challenge. Juliet begins to look a bit subdued, as if she might withdraw into herself. Rowena affirms her and offers support.

Rowena   You grasped the principles of planning very quickly. I am willing to help you develop a useful work plan if you will give it your attention.

Juliet   Yes, I do need to get more control over my load. Perhaps if I have a clearer idea of my commitments I will know what I can take on for others without becoming swamped.

PRACTISING FEEDBACK, SUPPORT AND CHALLENGE

These are skills that need practice, like many others. For some people, being challenging may require particular discipline, while for others it comes almost too easily. Exercise 20 provides a structure within which you can practise.

Exercise 20 – Practising feedback, support and challenge

1. Make an arrangement to work in a 'three' with people from your team. You can rotate the roles as shown in Exercise 12. You may need to find an arrangement that is sufficiently comfortable and safe, without being inappropriately cosy.
2. Each participant has a turn practising coaching for an agreed time, for example:
   - A coaches B   5 minutes
   - B gives feedback to A   2 minutes
   - Observer C gives feedback to A   3 minutes
3. Coaches, speaking from their knowledge of their pupils, give feedback on how they see them in their work. Include support and one or two challenges.
4. The pupils then give feedback to their coaches on the experience.
   - How well balanced was the session, between support and challenge?
   - Did the coach affirm the pupil?
   - Was the pupil supported in receiving the challenge(s)?
   - Was the coach clear?
   - Was the feedback owned?
   - Was the feedback specific?

Remember that it is possible that pupils may experience a session very differently from the observers (by only hearing some aspects, for example).

If a coach has not used a mix of support and challenge, check if this might be because the coach finds that type of intervention difficult. If so, the coach may need to practise more.

ACTION LIST

1. Reflect on which feedback you find easier to receive: positive or negative.
2. Reflect on how naturally your style of coaching includes affirmation, support and challenge. Which of these do you need to develop?
3. Arrange to practise these skills in a three, using Exercise 20.
4. Introduce your enhanced skills into your coaching practice.
5. Are there any situations in which your pupil(s) need to be challenged? How can you challenge them and support them?

PART 4

ADVANCED SKILLS

PART 4

In this part we shall look at the advanced skills coaches can develop once they have established the core skills.

KEY LEARNING POINTS

You will learn about:

- precision in language and how to use it to benefit your pupils
- resistance to your coaching and how to work with it to advantage
- the importance of the *process* of the session as distinct from its *content*
- the subtle and often unconscious processes present in the relationship between coach and pupil

In this section of the book I introduce some more advanced issues and coaching skills. I have kept these separate because I think it important that you first become familiar with the coaching practice already introduced. These topics are appropriate when you feel comfortable and relaxed with basic coaching, and are ready for more challenge yourself.

If you find your coaching running into difficulties or becoming stuck, you may want to consult this part of the book as a reference source. You may find here clues about what is happening in your sessions and gain help in moving things on.

CHAPTER 12

PRECISION IN LANGUAGE

A man does not know what he is saying until he knows what he is not saying.

G.K. Chesterton, *As I was Saying* (1936)

KEY LEARNING POINTS

In this chapter you will have the opportunity to learn about how:

- we commonly defocus our choice of words to soften our meaning
- we can invite pupils to sharpen language in order to help them find greater clarity
- we can encourage pupils to follow through to new thoughts and insights

INTRODUCTION

In everyday language we often use phrases or expressions that are vague, incorrect or that distort a meaning. We may use a euphemism when a more precise choice of phrase would be unpalatable. In recent years phrases such as 'friendly fire', 'collateral damage' and 'inoperatives' have come into the vocabulary.

In other instances we commonly distort our choice of phrase to reduce its impact or distance ourselves from its implications. In these ways we reduce the effectiveness of our communication, or cloud its impact on both others and ourselves

We defocus our language to soften its impact.

Superior coaches will notice such language and invite pupils to clarify such imprecision. Pupils then have the opportunity to reclaim their power and responsibility – literally response–ability, that is, their ability to respond and take action.

In this chapter I will introduce some of the common ways in which we distort language, and I will show how coaches can help pupils clarify their meaning.

Sharpening language helps identify issues.

Sharpening the precision of language can be very powerful and I want to include here a warning. Sometimes we use vague language to avoid facing an issue that would be unacceptable to us, perhaps for deeply personal reasons that are often not conscious. Superior coaches are respectful of such personal matters. They will help their pupils become aware of how they may disempower themselves in their work through their language. They also recognize that we all have 'tender spots', and they will respect their pupils' wisdom about what to tackle and what to leave alone. It is not the role of the coach to override this.

Just occasionally, when you invite pupils to sharpen their language they may refuse, or they may think they are doing so but unconsciously repeat the distorted phrase. It is important to respect this 'resistance', particularly if the focus is of a more personal nature. I will cover the issue of 'resistance' in Chapter 13.

GENERALIZATIONS

One common way in which we defocus our language is by using generalizations to avoid the specific. Generalizations are

By generalizing we avoid dealing with specifics.

less tangible – we can often do nothing about a matter in general. So, by generalizing, we may distance ourselves from the possibility of doing something about it.

Generalizations can take many forms, but use of the pronouns *one* or *you* when *I* would be more appropriate is often a clue. Inviting speakers to own the statement by using *I*, if that is what they mean, can help them focus on whether the matter does belong to them. If so, they can decide whether they wish to take responsibility for it.

John is coaching Rowena, and the subject has got around to how Rowena often ends up taking on tasks that she had expected her people to do.

Rowena   Often I end up working late, or even at weekends, to complete a report or something that's needed for a meeting. It's the price one has to pay for being a manager.

John   It sounds sort of inevitable.

Rowena   Yes, when one takes on responsibility, one has to pay the price.

John has noticed Rowena is generalizing, and decides to draw Rowena's attention to it.

John   I notice you are saying 'one' when talking about this inevitability. I suggest you own this and use 'I' rather than 'one'.

Rowena hesitates.

John   Try it.

Rowena   When I take on responsibility I have to pay a price ... that doesn't feel comfortable ... it's sort of true, but it feels odd ... I'm not sure that I want to be paying a price all the time.

Rowena's assumption was based on a generalization, which John has invited her to question. She has not resolved it, but she is now beginning to question and re-evaluate it. She starts to explore the implications.

Rowena   You have to take responsibility. You can't just let a report be late. If it's not been done on time you have to get it ready yourself.

John   I notice you are saying 'you' when I think you are talking about yourself. Try repeating that with 'I'.

Rowena   I have to take responsibility. I can't just let a report be late. If it's not been done on time I have to do it myself.

There is a silence for some moments while Rowena reflects on how this statement feels for her. It occurs to her that she might sometimes take on responsibility inappropriately, or in a way that takes responsibility away from her people.

MERGING

Another way we may distort language is by obscuring the boundary between ourselves as individuals and others. We may be unable to do anything about the whole, and by merging with it we can avoid the issue of whether we do anything ourselves about the particular.

When Queen Victoria did not like a joke she responded with the now famous phrase 'We are not amused'. In doing so she was merging her own taste with the entire court, and it would have been a strong person who disagreed and said 'Well, I think it's hilarious'. The royal 'we' can be used to anchor ourselves to a greater authority that cannot be questioned.

When someone uses 'we' they are speaking for the whole and are presuming some degree of shared values and responsibility. Some sharing of values is appropriate. Without it partnerships, teams or, indeed, organizations could not

By merging with others we may avoid taking responsibility.

exist. However, sometimes it is inappropriate in that it can hide individual responsibility and choice.

Long-established couples can lose their sense of separateness. Ask whether they want tea or coffee and they may glance at each other before one replies, 'We'll have coffee'. The possibility that they may choose individually and perhaps differently may have been lost in the interests of harmony.

Merging is often used to avoid the discomfort of dealing with differences. It is only when merging is broken that the differences can be addressed.

Rowena continues in her session with John, having reflected on whether she sometimes takes on responsibility inappropriately.

Rowena   You know, part of the problem is that we don't have enough time between the monthly returns coming in from the branch offices. We've got to trade off between the completeness of information and getting the reports ready to be available in time for the board meeting.

John is aware that there are different groups involved in this process, and he notices how Rowena is speaking for them all. It feels as if the whole system is unchangeable.

John   Who's 'we'?
Rowena   Well, the branch managers have to get their figures together in time, so that we, that's my lot, can prepare the summary report in time.
John   If any of the branches is late you come under pressure.
Rowena   Yes ... that's often the problem.

Rowena has started to separate the rather unaddressable 'we don't have enough time' into who is responsible for what.

Rowena   If they are late, I end up having to make up

> time for them . . . I sort of take responsibility for making up the time.
>
> **John** So, what do you want to do about this?
>
> **Rowena** Well, I guess I will have to spell out to the branches the latest date by which we must have the figures.

SWALLOWING WHOLE

A further way in which we give away our power to deal effectively with problems is by accepting something at face value, without adequately evaluating it for ourselves. It then becomes a 'given truth' or 'introjection' that we have difficulty questioning.

In early life we have to learn how to manage in the world. We are given a number of rules by our parents or other carers, which we have to accept. This may have been reinforced in our education, particularly where much of it has focused on cramming in information. Later in life we need to learn to evaluate or 'chew on' what we are offered to see whether it is right for us rather than swallowing it unquestioningly. Otherwise we may accept too readily what we are told, particularly if it comes from an authority figure.

Accepting without question is more appropriate in early life than in adulthood.

One clue that can point to introjection is the use of 'ought' or 'should'. This may imply that the thought or action is imposed rather than truly the speaker's.

> Rowena continues to reflect on the problems she meets when the branches are late submitting their figures.
>
> **Rowena** OK, so I can spell out to the branches when they need to get their figures in, but they're busy. They will probably be late anyway. I ought to be able to cope with that.
>
> **John** So even after you've said when the figures need

> to be in, you anticipate there will be lateness, and that you will have to manage with this.
>
> **Rowena** Yes, If I am doing my job properly my department should be able to cope.
>
> **John** Who says you should be able to cope and make up for other departments' lateness?
>
> **Rowena** Well ... I do, I suppose ... if I am doing my job properly, I should be able to get the report together on time.
>
> **John** I notice you are using 'should' quite a lot. I am wondering whether you are feeling under an expectation?
>
> **Rowena** You've told me how important it is that the report is available for the board meeting – so yes, I think you do expect that.
>
> John is aware that six months ago Rowena's department was having difficulty collating the figures and producing the summary; he had told her to sort it out and not to give him excuses. He wanted Rowena to take more responsibility for her people's work. Now he wonders whether she is taking on responsibility for more than her area.
>
> **John** Do you think that's reasonable?
>
> **Rowena** Well, yes, insofar as the process of preparing the report from the figures is concerned, but I don't have any control over whether the branches send in their figures on time.
>
> Now Rowena has started to separate what is her responsibility and what is not.

SEQUENCING

Often we do not follow through to a conclusion.

Often we stop short of following a thought process through to its conclusion. Sometimes this may be because we imagine that the outcome will be uncomfortable. We omit or delete the conclusion. This practice is very widespread, and widely accepted by casual listeners. If we followed our thinking through to its conclusion, we would need to change a great deal in our lives, our work and the world at large.

Spotting deletions takes a bit of practice. One clue is if the listener feels unsatisfied, as if something is missing or incomplete. You can invite speakers to complete their thoughts by using a prompt such as 'because?'.

Rowena is still reflecting on the boundaries of her responsibilities.

Rowena It's all very well, but I can't just say the report is late because the branches are late with their figures.

John feels dissatisfied with this statement, as if it is not the whole story. He decides to probe further:

John   Because?
Rowena Because … its going to reflect badly …

Here the deletion is obvious, almost as if the sentence has been cut short. John invites its completion.

John   Reflect badly on?
Rowena (hesitating then adding) On the branches.

A variation of completing truncated thinking is to invite exploration of a further thought sequence to see where it goes.

John	And if the branches are seen to be late with their figures ...
Rowena	I will feel I have let them down.
John	This really makes me aware of how much you take on responsibility for protecting the branches from their problems, and how much pressure you put on yourself and your people as a consequence.

PRACTISE WORKING WITH PRECISION

Use Exercise 21 to develop your awareness of language.

Exercise 21 – Practise working with precision

Arrange practice sessions in your pair or three. The person in the role of pupil chooses a topic to explore. The coach listens to the language being used and, when appropriate, draws attention to:

1. Generalizations – encourage use of 'I' rather than 'one' or 'you'.
2. Merging – encourage use of 'I' rather than 'we'.
3. Swallowing whole – explore use of 'should' or 'ought'.
4. Sequencing – spot deletions and encourage their completion and the follow-through of the pupil's thinking.

In these practice sessions, take more risk in experimenting with these skills than you might wish to do in a 'real' session.

Discuss how helpful or otherwise the sharpening of language has been.

ACTION LIST

1. Start listening to the precision in the language you hear around you.
2. Start noticing when 'we', 'you' or 'one' is used when it may be inappropriate.
3. Start noticing how 'should' and 'ought' is used. When does it seem appropriate, and when might it be inappropriate?
4. Practise your use of language using Exercise 21.
5. Listen in your coaching sessions and, when it feels appropriate, help your pupils explore the precision of their language.

CHAPTER 13

RESISTANCE

You can take a horse to the water, but you cannot make it drink.

Proverb

KEY LEARNING POINTS

In this chapter you will have the opportunity to learn about:

- the importance of resistance
- how trying to overcome resistance is flawed
- how to work with resistance
- the role of polar opposites

INTRODUCTION

Sometimes the people we are trying to help may seem to resist the help we offer. Perhaps it is obvious to us what they should do, and yet they seem reluctant to act. There are varying levels of pressure we may apply.

1. At the gentlest level, we might direct them towards what we think they need to do. Yet they do not take it up, as if they cannot see what to us is so obvious.
2. Alternatively, we may let them know what we think they should be doing, and yet they seem reluctant to take it on.

Perhaps it does not seem such a good idea to them, or it appears as if they will only do it if we press them.

3. At the strongest level, we can be direct and tell them what they should do. Often the approach or initiative that seemed so obvious or promising to us does not prove so fruitful in their hands. Perhaps it encounters delays, problems arise, or there is a lack of energy for driving the strategy through. Perhaps it seems it would be simpler to do it ourselves.

All these scenarios are demonstrating a very important phenomenon: resistance. In this chapter we shall look at the significance of resistance, and introduce some ways of working with it.

THE SIGNIFICANCE OF RESISTANCE

When we meet with resistance, our natural inclination may be to increase the pressure we are applying in order to overcome the resistance we are experiencing in the other person. We may doubt whether we have explained our reasoning clearly enough, and try again. When this fails we may begin to wonder whether this person really is 'on our side' or just being difficult. We may even be drawn into applying more pressure, perhaps using threats, albeit indirectly. In some organizational cultures the issue may become an open trial of strength. In less open organizations we may resort to indirect attempts to manipulate things our way. In any event, the objective is to make the person behave the way we want them to, despite his or her resistance.

Applying more pressure to overcome resistance is fundamentally flawed. There is a law of physics that states that for every force there is an equal and opposite force. So it is with resistance – the more we push, the more resistance we meet. Resistance can be direct, but often it appears indirectly. The initiatives we set up somehow do not deliver the results we expected. Problems are encountered, or staff move on, etc.

In such cases we are missing an important truth:

When we try to overcome resistance we will be opposed.

Resistance points us to the problem that needs to be addressed.
Resistance is such an important clue that we should value it
and appreciate it, rather than regard it as something to be
overcome. Even if we manage to overcome it we shall miss
the truth it is showing us, and the problem will probably show
up in some other form.

I have come to value resistance so fundamentally that if I
come across none, I begin to feel suspicious. Why is there no
resistance? Where has it gone? How is it going to show up
later?

Superior coaches understand the importance of
resistance and its value. They work with the resistance they
meet, to help their pupils discover their options and the path
of action that is right for them. This requires the superior
coach to be genuinely open about the possible outcomes. If
we attempt to appear open and non-directive about something we are not open about, we are trying to use coaching
skills to manipulate our pupils. This will destroy trust and
inevitably fail in the long run. If we as coaches have a need for
a particular outcome, perhaps because of a management role
that we also have, it is better to be clear and up-front about
this.

Resistance is a vital pointer to where attention is needed.

AWARENESS

In Chapter 2, I introduced the view that people are self-
motivated, given sufficient information. One of the simplest
reasons a coach may experience a pupil 'resisting' is that the
pupil may lack information or awareness about the options
available to them. The task of the coach may therefore be to
focus not on overcoming this resistance, nor on changing
minds, but on helping pupils become more aware of their
options. The superior coach trusts that when pupils are fully
aware of their options, then they will take a course of action
that is right for them.

Helping pupils develop awareness of their options is helpful.

Rowena is coaching Mike. Mike is the production manager, and has responsibility for the publications once they have been handed over from the editor. He subcontracts both printing and despatch. The last two issues have been delayed at the printers and in the last issue there was a batch in which some pages were collated upside-down. Rowena and Mike have been exploring the facts involved, and Rowena wonders why Mike does not just change printers. Rowena summarizes:

Rowena So, despite your talk with PrintRight when they were late with the February issue, they were late again with March's. Then after that was finally despatched, you were appalled to discover some of the copies were faulty. You feel things are going from bad to worse.

Mike Yes. I've been on to Roger at PrintRight to complain again, but I am beginning to dread that they will screw up again with April's issue, which is due to go to them next week.

Rowena I wonder why you don't just change printers.

Mike It's not as simple as that – I can't just switch like that.

Rowena senses Mike is resisting her invitation to consider switching. She could try convincing him, or even lean on him to give it a go. However, she is aware of the pitfalls of this. Not least of these is that if Mike switches and there are then some problems, he will probably feel these are now of her making and he will not be fully committed to solving them. Rowena focuses on Mike's resistance and her need to increase his awareness of it.

Rowena So what are your options?

Mike Well, I can have another meeting with Mike. I can warn him that we will not tolerate a repeat of the mess last time. Maybe I need to look at the penalty clauses in our contract to see if I can have more clout with them.

Rowena   Those both sound good things to try. And I notice you have not also included the possibility of switching printers.

Mike   Last time we tried that, before your time, it was a nightmare. It was so bad that we went back to PrintRight after failing to get an issue out at all.

Rowena   If you were to switch again, how would you want to manage it?

Mike   Well, I would want to see the new lot do at least a dummy run ... taking the DTP file and preparing a minimal print run. And before relying on them I would want to institute a quality sampling step between them and the despatchers.

Rowena   So you are reluctant to switch printers because of your past experience, and if you were to do so, you would want to prepare for it very carefully.

Mike now sees switching is one of his options. His experience shows he needs to plan it properly. He decides to explore the possible alternatives and to let Roger know that he is doing so. He still feels the decision to switch would be his.

WORKING WITH RESISTANCE

So far in this chapter I have stressed that trying to overcome resistance is fundamentally flawed. Either our attempts to do so will themselves be resisted, or the issue behind the resistance will show up in some other form. There will be a kind of impasse.

One of the most powerful and helpful ways of working with resistance is literally, to work *with* the resistance, that is, not only to accept and allow it but actively to encourage it. Superior coaches recognize that when pupils appear to resist, the pupils are expressing an important truth for them. By

Instead of fighting against resistance, work with it.

encouraging pupils in their exploration, the coach supports them so they can stop using energy to oppose attempts to get them to change and can instead apply it to exploring their truth. When they have done this, they will be free to form a balanced view of what action is appropriate.

This approach is paradoxical. It may take you a little while to gain confidence in it, but paradox is an extremely powerful way of helping people.

When coaches work with resistance, the aim is to allow pupils to explore fully the advantages of their present approach. Without needing to use energy to defend this position, pupils can perhaps go further than before in this exploration. This breaks the impasse and helps the pupils find a broader perspective.

Sometimes, with support for their resistance, pupils will build up their position to an extent that it becomes untenable and the whole position collapses. Imagine a child is building a tower with wooden bricks but for some reason they cannot continue doing so. Perhaps it is time for bed, or maybe the tower is in the way of something else. You could try taking it down. The child will probably resist, perhaps by adding bricks as fast as you take them down. It becomes a trial of strength. If you force the issue, the child will feel thwarted and angry and perhaps be reluctant to settle for the night. An alternative is to help the child build the tower higher and higher, until eventually the tower collapses. The child has discovered the limits of the game and has completed its play.

Paradox is powerful.

Looked at another way, if you want to travel east but it is problematic, it may be easier to go west. If you go west far enough you will end up in the east.

Rowena continues her coaching session with Mike. Mike is still reluctant to switch printers, and Rowena is beginning to wonder why this is so.

Rowena Tell me, Mike, what are the advantages of staying with PrintRight?

| Mike | Well, they've been doing our printing for three years now. We've built up rather a good working relationship with them. They understand the feel of the publication. They have even corrected the odd error that has slipped through our proofing. |

Rowena decides to encourage Mike further.

Rowena	Sounds like they are almost part of the team.
Mike	Yes, and I really get on with Roger. He seems to understand our problems well. When we have been late he has often managed to accommodate that and help us catch up. There was an issue last autumn, November I think, which we would never have got out on time if Roger had not turned it round in less than the agreed two weeks.
Rowena	In what other ways has Roger been helpful?
Mike	Well, remember just before Christmas we found the dates in the calendar for the next year were wrong? We had already sent PrintRight the copy, and they had already done their set-up and had just started the print run when I contacted Roger. He was really obliging, stopped the run, took the corrections over the phone and sorted it out. Otherwise it would have been a disaster.
Rowena	It sounds helpful – a sort of mutual back-scratching.
Mike	Yes, it is really.
Rowena	So how can you help Roger – to scratch his back, as it were?
Mike	Well, when they were going to be late in January I had a word with the distributors, and they were able to make up the time.
Rowena	And how can you help Roger now?
Mike	Well … I guess I have to be understanding

when they are being late, like this month ... and last. [Pauses] Hell, where does this end?

Rowena has encouraged Mike to explore the advantages of his relationship with Roger, and in doing so Mike realizes that he may have compromised his relationship with his sub-contractor.

POLAR OPPOSITES

With any situation we may have a range of possible responses or styles. However, we may constrain ourselves by only using a subset of the possibilities. The other possibilities are not available to us because we are unaware of them, or because they are unfamiliar or too uncomfortable for us.

Superior coaches recognize that pupils have a wider range of abilities than they are using at present. They support and encourage them to explore the alternatives without any expectation that the pupils should adopt a particular style.

Consider the case of Mike that we have been following in this chapter. Mike's style has been to build a rather comfortable relationship with Roger that has suited them both but may have compromised Mike's position. Rowena is wondering what other styles Mike could use but which he may avoid because they are uncomfortable or unfamiliar to him. We may conjecture the extreme polarities shown in Figure 13.1.

Exploring opposite extreme positions develops awareness.

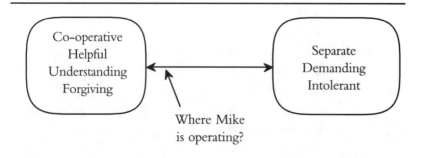

FIGURE 13.1: Possible polarities of Mike's style

At this stage it is only conjecture, and it is important that Rowena allow Mike to find his own actual polarities and explore them. Then he will be freer to adopt a wider range of styles, rather than operating habitually in one particular way.

In the spirit of working with resistance, it is usually most helpful to encourage pupils to explore fully the polarity with which they are most comfortable. From this place they may discover their opposite polarity.

Rowena   Perhaps it would be helpful for you to really explore the benefits of your working relationship with Roger. If you were to really go with this, how could you help each other even more?

Mike   Well, I think I have to keep some balance in it ... so that I still have some control over the situation.

Rowena   Maybe, but I suggest you let go of that for now. Try exploring how mutually helpful you could be to each other.

Mike   Well ... if I really get into that, it would make some things a lot easier. Even if we were late I could send Roger the copy we have so far. He could start work on it, and then I could send him updates as we made them, over the telephone even. Hey ... we could even dictate late items to him! We wouldn't have to worry about proofing, page fit or any of that! [Pause] Actually, it would be a bit like him being one of the staff working at the printers.

Mike reflects for some moments on this scenario, and then continues.

Mike   The problem would be that he doesn't work for me, and I would have no real control. If there were errors it would not be clear where the responsibility lay ... and I have no control over how he spends his time. I think it's important that we have editorial control in-house, and that we have a clear contract with the printers.

Rowena sees Mike's exploration has helped him identify an opposite polarity, and she invites him to explore this.

Rowena OK Mike, I suggest you now forget your comfortable working relationship with Roger, and explore what it would be like to have a strictly contractual and more distant relationship.

Mike Mmm ... well, that's difficult because I think some cooperation is important.

Rowena Just for now I suggest you suspend that part and see what it's like to have a less cosy relationship.

Mike Ooh ... if I really did that ... umm ... it feels odd ...

Rowena Just give it a go.

Mike 'Roger ... you're late with this month's print run. And you were late with the last one. It's not good enough! I am not going to be messed about like this. You've blown it ... I shall take my business elsewhere.' Actually, yes I do feel fed up with him. I guess he would plead for another chance.

Rowena How might you respond to him from this extreme position?

Mike 'Too late! You had a chance to get back after last time. Finished! Gone! That's it! Goodbye!' Wow ... that's a powerful position to be in. [Pauses] It also leaves me 'up the creek without a paddle'. I would have next month's issue to get out with no printer lined up.

Rowena senses Mike has now stretched his awareness of his possible approaches to their extreme poles. He now needs to find his ability to operate flexibly over the range.

Rowena So you've visited the two extreme approaches you could take. How might you want to handle it in practice?

Mike I think I need to spell out to Roger that I cannot have the printing late like this. I appreciate our working relationship but we must achieve the issue dates. If he is late again, I will have to try alternatives. I think it might be good to speak to a couple of other printers in advance, and see if they will do a dummy run for us so we know whether they could take over. I think I might let Roger know that's what I am doing.

Rowena has helped Mike explore the poles of his possible approaches, and now he is finding a more flexible approach. He is both valuing the importance of a good working relationship but is also able to use the contractual relationship to demand a satisfactory service.

PRACTISE WORKING WITH RESISTANCE

Use Exercise 22 to practise working with resistance.

Exercise 22 – Practise working with resistance

Arrange practice sessions in your pair or three.

1. The person in the role of pupil chooses a topic that he or she finds difficult and wishes to explore.
2. The coach listens for the pupil's resistance and encourages the pupil to develop his or her resistance even more, or to take that view much further.

   In these practice sessions, take more risk in experimenting with these skills than you might wish to do in a 'real' session.
3. When giving feedback, the observer can note in what ways

the coach might have encouraged the pupil to go even further with his or her resistance.

4. Discuss how helpful or otherwise it has been to go with resistance.

ACTION LIST

1. In your coaching sessions, start listening for 'resistance'.
2. Remind yourself that 'resistance' is not something to be overcome but is an important pointer to what needs to be explored.
3. Practise working with resistance and polarities using Exercise 22.
4. Start helping your pupils become more aware of the advantages to them of their present approach.
5. Encourage your pupils to explore the extreme polarities of their options.

CHAPTER 14

PROCESS

Recognize what is before your eyes, and what is hidden
will be revealed to you.

Gospel of Thomas

KEY LEARNING POINTS

In this chapter you will have the opportunity to learn about:

- the distinction between content and process
- working with a pupil's process
- process-focused interventions

INTRODUCTION

So far in this book I have introduced coaching as an approach
in which pupils, or sometimes coaches, identify a problem.
Coaches then help pupils develop their awareness and skills so
that they can address and make progress on the identified
issue.

While this is a valuable and important aspect of coaching,
it can mask an even more important and potent type of
learning. If pupils learn how to make progress with the
identified problem, there is progress. However, because it is
the *problem* that is addressed, we can expect the pupils to be
back with the next problem, and so on.

Even greater improvement in performance comes about when the pupil learns not just about the problem but about what it was in the pupil's style that led to it being a problem in the first place. Potentially pupils then have the opportunity to deal in future with a whole class of issues without each one becoming a problem requiring coaching. Superior coaches will therefore want to be aware of their pupils' *process* and not just the *content* of the problems they bring to the coach.

In this chapter we look at how coaches can recognize the style of their pupils and work with their underlying process, rather than just focusing on the session content.

> Coaches need to distinguish process from content.

IDENTIFYING PROCESS

It is all too easy for coaches to become so engrossed in helping their pupils solve problems that they fail to attend to the process. It is important that coaches, while attending to the identified problem, are also monitoring the process as well. Once you have experience of several pupils you will be able to recognize their particular styles, and their styles point to their underlying processes. Table 14.1 presents a checklist for identifying a pupil's style. It is not exclusive – you may wish to make additions of your own.

> It is all too easy to become so involved in content that we miss the process.

TABLE 14.1: Some indicators of style

The following can point to a pupil's style:

1. Does this issue form a pattern with similar issues that this pupil has brought to you?
2. What stands out as characteristic to this pupil compared with other individuals?
3. Might the issue not have been a problem or not arisen with a different individual?
4. How might this pupil have contributed to the occurrence of this issue?
5. What are the advantages to this pupil of having this issue?

Now use Exercise 23 to identify the styles of a pupil of yours. Consider not just styles you may see as 'problems' but also those you see as 'strengths'.

Exercise 23 – Identifying pupils' styles

Take ten minutes to reflect on coaching sessions you have had with one of your pupils. Use sessions from one pupil only.

1. Use the checklist in Table 14.1 to identify possible style issues for this pupil.
2. Write these down – you will need these points later for Exercise 24.
3. Now consider whether there are any other style issues for this pupil.
4. What additional checklist items might you add to the list in Table 14.1 to help you identify these additional styles?

The above exercise invites you to think about what may be a pupil's style in general, rather than a unique response to one particular situation. If what you are beginning to see does reflect this pupil's style, then the chances are that this style will also be reflected in how the pupil interacts with you in coaching sessions. As an example, suppose that a pupil has a tendency to be unclear about what action is required following a meeting. This tendency may also show up during coaching sessions in a lack of clarity about the actions agreed in the coaching sessions.

The parallel processes can give you insight in both directions. You may sense a possible difficulty in the way the pupil operates 'out there', and this may help you to identify how the same difficulty is likely to arise 'in here'. Alternatively, your experience of the pupil 'in here' may help you spot what is going on 'out there'. For example if you see that a pupil is unclear about actions following your coaching sessions, it raises the possibility that this pupil is unclear about actions in his or her work 'out there'.

Working with process is a very powerful opportunity for learning.

This has very important implications. First, while such difficulties remain unaddressed not only may they continue to make the pupil less effective 'out there', but they may well make the coaching sessions ineffective 'in here'. It may be essential to address this before progress can be made. Second, the coaching sessions may provide the best learning ground on which the pupil can become more effective. For example, rather than coaching the pupil to be clearer about agreeing actions 'out there', it will probably be more effective to coach the pupil in dealing effectively with actions 'in here'. This is a live learning situation, and it provides an opportunity for the most profound and fundamental learning.

Exercise 24 – Identifying a pupil's process

Take ten minutes to reflect on a pupil's process. Using the list that you prepared in Exercise 23, consider how each of the styles you have identified manifests in your coaching sessions with this pupil.

1. Consider the strengths of this pupil's work 'out there'. How do these manifest in your coaching sessions?
2. Consider the difficulties the pupil experiences in their work 'out there'. How are these manifested in your coaching sessions? Could they be limiting the effectiveness of the sessions?

Reflect on your experience of this pupil in your coaching sessions.

1. What strengths do you see in the sessions that the pupil may not be using 'out there'?
2. What problems have you experienced in your work with this pupil? How does this inform you about what may be happening 'out there'?

WORKING WITH PROCESS

Once you are aware of process issues, you can help pupils explore their process and learn from it. The skill is to do this in a way that is helpful and constructive for the pupil. Remember that, while there may be some truth in what you see as the process issue, the pupil may have a different view of it.

It is easy to be or appear critical and destructive. For example, a coach might suspect that the pupil has contributed to the problem being presented. To say 'No one else would have had this problem – what have you done to create it?' is

Working with process is an important skill that needs to be learnt.

hardly likely to engender confidence and trust. On the other hand something like: 'You've identified how X has contributed to this situation. How might you have done things differently?' is more balanced and unthreatening. Working with process is a form of feedback, and you should be familiar with the feedback skills presented in Chapter 11.

The simplest way of working with process is to encourage your pupils to become aware themselves of their process, or to offer your awareness without implying criticism.

Table 14.2 offers some possible interventions that can be used to develop awareness of each of the styles in Table 14.1.

TABLE 14.2: Possible process interventions

1. Does this issue form a pattern with similar issues this pupil has brought?
   - *Is this sort of problem familiar to you?*
   - *Where else have you met with this sort of issue?*
2. What stands out as characteristic for this pupil compared with other individuals?
   - *How might you have handled this differently?*
3. Might the issue not have been a problem or not arisen with a different individual?
   - *How might others have done this?*
   - *I imagine that if someone else had been handling this, different issues might have arisen. What might have been different?*
4. How might this pupil have contributed to the occurrence of this issue?
   - *How might you have contributed to this process?*
5. What are the advantages to this pupil of having this issue?
   - *What has been the advantage for you of handling it this way?*
   - *What have you gained through this situation?*

As I have said before, working with the pupil's process as it manifests itself in the coaching session is one of the most powerful ways, perhaps *the* most powerful way, of enabling the pupil to develop effectiveness. It involves:

■ helping pupils discover how their process manifests in the actual coaching session;
■ helping the pupil find a way of being more effective in the session here and now.

When pupils make these changes or find new ways of working here and now, it opens up a natural way for them to make the same changes 'out there'.

ROWENA TURNS TO PROCESS

In Chapter 6 you followed Rowena as she coached Pierre to help him deal with the erratic variations in his financial balance. You may recall he had resolved to set up a meeting with Brian and Juliet to discuss how their decisions caused these variations. Now we join Rowena at her next session with Pierre.

Rowena is on the phone when there is a soft knock on her door and Pierre looks round. He sees Rowena is on the phone and withdraws. After Rowena has finished her call she goes to fetch Pierre in.

Pierre   Hello ... is it convenient for our session now? I could come back later.

Rowena   Oh ... er ... come on in, Pierre.

As the coaching proceeds they look at the actions Pierre took from the last session.

Pierre   I've not been able to make much progress on the issues we discussed last time. I set up the meeting with Brian and Juliet, but then there was the problem Juliet had with that advertiser, and we didn't get our meeting.

Rowena   What happened exactly?

Pierre   Well, Juliet was being harassed by the advertiser and didn't have time for our meeting, and Brian had to rework his editorial to introduce an extra news item. All round it just wasn't possible.

Rowena   Everybody seems to have been too busy to fit your meeting in.

Pierre   Yes, it does seem that way.

Rowena begins to realize that this may be a pattern with Pierre.

Rowena   Is that something familiar to you ... that people are often too busy to give you their time?

Pierre   Oh yes. Well, everybody is very busy.

Rowena   What did you notice when we met just now?

Pierre   Nothing, really. You were busy on the phone.

Rowena   I remember you checking if it was convenient. I think you offered to come back later. Actually, I nearly took you up on that.

Pierre   Well, if you are that busy I can come back. It's no trouble.

Rowena   Pierre – notice what has happened in this session. You saw I was busy and offered to postpone our meeting. I had a strong temptation to take you up on your offer. Now when I refer to it you are again offering to postpone. I recall something similar happened at the beginning of our last session. Juliet and Brian were both busy, but how might you have contributed to the postponement of your meeting?

Pierre   Perhaps I was rather ready to accept a postponement?

Rowena   Perhaps. My experience of you just now was that you rather invited me to postpone our meeting.

Pierre   Maybe I have to be more assertive.

Rowena   OK, well just now you offered to stop this meeting. What do you want to do about that now?

[Rowena is creating an opportunity for Pierre to confirm his learning in the here-and-now of the session.]

Pierre [hesitates] Would it be OK if we continue our session?

Rowena notices she still does not feel like giving Pierre time. She realizes her experience of him is central to this issue, and she decides to stay with it.

Rowena I notice you are making it very easy for me to cancel it. I'm not inclined to make time for you unless you are more convincing. Try stating what you want!

Pierre [speaking more strongly] I know you are busy, but I would really like to continue with our session as arranged. There are other issues I need to raise.

Rowena Ah! That sounds clear. Yes, I am busy, but I hear you want the session and I now feel willing to give you the time.

Pierre I have to be clearer when I want a meeting to happen, and not be so ready to have it cancelled ... or even invite its cancellation.

Pierre has taken the step of being clear and becoming more effective in the coaching session itself. Through this he is likely also to become more effective 'out there' in his job. This learning is more powerful than if Rowena had simply led him to resolve to be clearer, without him experiencing the change within the session.

ACTION LIST

1. Make sure you are familiar with the distinction between content and process.
2. Reflect on the style of one of your pupils. Use Exercise 23 for this.
3. Reflect on how the pupil's style shapes not just how the pupil works 'out there' on the job, but also in the coaching sessions with you. Use Exercise 24.
4. Start to draw your pupils' attention to their style and how it appears in the coaching sessions as well as 'out there'.

CHAPTER 15

RELATIONSHIP

Each of us really understands in others only those
feelings he is capable of producing himself.

André Gide, *Journal of 'The Counterfeiters'* (1921)

KEY LEARNING POINTS

In this chapter you will have the opportunity to learn about:

- the relationship between coach and pupil
- how the relationship is influenced by previous client experience
- how the relationship is influenced by previous coach experience
- how the coach's feelings can provide important insights into what is happening in the relationship

INTRODUCTION

In this part of the book we have been exploring the more advanced skills that coaches can use when working with pupils. In Chapter 14 we saw how a coaching session has potential for more than just dealing with the material presented by the pupil. There is potential for fundamental learning within the session itself.

In this chapter we take this a step further and look more

closely at the relationship between coach and pupil.

In the first section we shall look at the nature of the coach/pupil relationship. I will then introduce some of the complex and subtle ways in which the relationship can both enhance and inhibit the coaching process.

The main problem is that these processes frequently arise unconsciously and coach or pupil may be quite unaware of what is happening. While these processes remain outside of awareness they can be quite destructive to the relationship and hence to the coaching work. Once you can recognize these processes they will no longer be such a problem, and you can use your awareness of them to help the progress of the work.

Relationship issues are often unconscious.

THE COACH/PUPIL RELATIONSHIP

When two people work together there is something else present – the relationship between the two of them. One plus one makes more than two.

This is always true, even when the relationship is apparently minimal. Imagine two people who share a work space but who never communicate and ignore each other. There is a relationship even here, albeit a cold and frosty one. Their working life is influenced and shaped by this, and is different from what they would have if they worked alone.

The relationship is always present.

Relating is one of our most fundamental needs, along with food and warmth. Just as nutritionists may claim 'we are what we eat', many psychologists hold that 'we are our relationships'.

ECHOES FROM THE PUPIL'S PAST

When coach and pupil meet it is not an equal relationship. The coach is there to help the pupil, and the pupil is there to be helped. This is an asymmetrical relationship in which the coach is usually seen as holding more power than the pupil. The pupil is likely, therefore, to see the coach, to a greater or lesser extent, as an authority figure. This may be true regardless of whether the coach encourages or discourages such a view. It is a view the pupil will, often unconsciously, create of the coach.

In handling this situation the pupil is likely to call upon previous experience of relating to authority figures. This could be a previous boss, or perhaps a school teacher. Even those relationships will be based on yet earlier experiences. How we handle such relationships will be shaped by our formative experience of authority with our primary carers, usually our parents.

Pupils may bring past experiences into their relationship with the coach.

We are likely to transfer our early experience of authority figures onto those we see as in authority now. Our experience of them now may obviously or subtly echo for us our earlier experiences. This transference can be difficult to spot because it is unconscious. Unidentified it can be destructive.

In Chapter 14 (page 140) we followed a coaching session between Rowena and Pierre. Notice how deferential Pierre was, and how anxious he was not to trouble Rowena if she was busy. This stood out for Rowena as different from her experience of others, so there may be something particular about Pierre's life experience that makes him so cautious about Rowena. It would be inappropriate and presumptuous to think we can know what this was about, but we can surmise that Pierre has primary experience of someone being too busy to give him time. Further, as he is so anxious about intruding, it is likely that his experience of asking for time was not a happy one. As I write this I have an image of Pierre wanting his mother's attention, and she, perhaps worn down by other demands on her, shouting at him to go away. Although Pierre may have buried this hurtful memory long ago, its echo has perhaps reappeared in his relationship with Rowena.

The coaching session is not the appropriate place to get into such deep and personal material, and such work is beyond the scope of this book. However, wise coaches will be aware that the transference process is common and that we all transfer feelings to some extent. They will therefore be aware that transference is probably around for their pupils at some level, even if only subtly. When pupils seem to be having

Transference issues may be deeply personal.

difficulty in their relationship with a coach, the coach can remember that there may be a transference issue. That very awareness on the part of the coach will change the relationship and can ease the coaching process.

Rowena is meeting with Brian, the magazine editor. Brian is talking about how he often needs to exercise editorial control over articles submitted for the magazine, and how the original authors do not always like the changes or cuts that he has made in their submissions.

Brian   Sometimes I have to reduce the length of an article ... we don't have unlimited space. Besides, some people repeat themselves quite unnecessarily.

Rowena You are taking editorial responsibility.

Brian   Yes, that's right, but then they complain about the changes I've made.

Rowena's experience of Brian is that he sometimes seems rather autocratic. She starts to invite him to explore different ways of working with authors.

Rowena I wonder if there are ways of letting authors know why you have had to make the changes.

Brian   You see ... nobody's happy with what I do.

Rowena notes that Brian did not pick up her invitation to explore but made a rather general comment. She is unsure what to do with it and decides to clarify.

Rowena You say 'nobody's happy'. Who do you mean? Who is not happy with what you do?

Brian hesitates.

Rowena Who are you thinking of right now that is not happy with what you do?

Brian   Well ... you for one ...

Rowena   You say that I'm not happy with your work, but I didn't say that. Actually I think you do the editing very well [affirms]. I did note your need to address how you work with authors. I asked what other ways there might be of letting them know about changes you have made.

Brian is silent for a while, as if he does not know how to handle this.

Rowena   I am struck by how you heard me as critical just now. Is feeling criticized familiar to you?

Brian   Yes, I'm always being criticized. When I worked on the evening paper my boss was always criticizing me ... it was intolerable.

Rowena   And is that experience more widespread for you?

Brian   [Reflects for a moment] I was always being criticized at school, by teachers.

Rowena surmises that feeling criticized may be part of Brian's life experience and that there may be echoes of the past in his experience of her.

Rowena   What I said was intended to be helpful, and I was not being critical. But I do recognize that you heard it as a criticism. Perhaps you are expecting criticism and are sometimes over-ready to hear it.

ECHOES FROM THE COACH'S PAST

In the previous section I have described how a pupil may transfer onto the coach qualities experienced in earlier relationships, and that this can unconsciously condition the pupil's relationship with the coach.

There can also be a 'flip-side' to this process: that the pupil, or the way that the pupil behaves, resonates within the

Coaches also transfer experience into the relationship.

coach and brings up feelings or impulses that do not really belong in the present. The coach is transferring his or her experience onto the pupil. To distinguish this 'flip-side' from the pupil's transference we shall refer to it as 'counter-transference'.

Returning again to Rowena and Pierre's session, recall how Rowena hesitated and nearly accepted Pierre's invitation to go away. It may be, of course, that she was just busy, but later she told him she had a 'strong temptation' to send him away. As Pierre took on the manner of a little boy getting under her feet, might Rowena have been tempted to get the space that she found so difficult to maintain for herself as a mother?

Such complications will always be present in the work of a coach, even if only at a very subtle level. Sometimes they will become significant and interfere with the coaching process. While counter-transference remains unconscious it can be a serious problem, not just for the coach but for the pupil as well, and can render the coaching relationship ineffective. Once the coach becomes aware of such an issue, it will usually cease to be a problem and dissolve. The difficulty is spotting what is an unconscious and subtle process.

Wise coaches know and understand that counter-transference may be around, whether they are aware of it or not. Certainly, if they experience strong reactions to a pupil they will consider whether they may be experiencing counter-transference. Wise coaches will reflect from time to time on how their relationships with their pupils may be influenced in ways of which they are not yet aware. The best place for this is when they are being coached themselves in their coaching work.

Rowena is continuing her session with Brian, or rather, trying to. She notices that she is feeling irritated by him. For a moment she is drawn to the idea of just finishing the session and telling him to sort things out by himself. She realizes that she is rather more than irritated – she may even be feeling angry with him. As she reflects on this she notes that Brian has not done anything to justify her being angry. She suddenly recalls that she was also tempted to send Pierre away. She becomes aware that 'sending people away' may be a way she copes with feeling angry with people, and that Brian has triggered this in her.

As she realizes this, her irritation with Brian himself subsides. She now feels more able to continue and she decides not to bring these personal issues of hers into the session with him.

EXPERIENCING ON BEHALF OF THE PUPIL

Sometimes a coach may find coaching with a particular pupil hard work. Perhaps the coach begins to dread the sessions, feels tired during the sessions, or frustrated with the intractability of the pupil. The situation may begin to feel intolerably difficult.

It can be very tempting for the coach to decide that these sessions are just not getting anywhere. The coach may be tempted to drop them, or perhaps pass the pupil on to someone else.

Wise coaches will reflect on whether they may be experiencing an echo from their own past – counter-transference. If this does not seem to be the case, they need to be open to the possibility that they may be experiencing something on behalf of the pupil. The pupil may be having difficulty not just in his or her work but in communicating that difficulty to the coach. Perhaps it seems impossible to describe, or perhaps too risky. For example, a pupil who is beginning to despair of sorting out a problem may feel too vulnerable to say so to the coach, particularly if that coach is also his or her manager.

What may happen is that the pupil may engender these same feelings in the coach as a way of communicating them. The coach, for example, may begin to feel despair with the pupil, either in the sense of 'alongside the pupil' or 'at the pupil'. While such feelings remain unconscious they can be disabling and destructive to the coaching process. Wise coaches listen regularly to their own reactions and feelings about the process of a session, and draw on it for guidance.

I may, for instance, be feeling frustrated with my pupil. As I become aware of this I can reflect on whether the pupil's situation is frustrating. I might offer: 'I imagine this situation is frustrating', or 'I notice I feel frustrated – I wonder if that's what it's like for you'.

When pupils are unable to express themselves, they may arrange for the coach to do it for them.

Rowena is continuing her session with Brian. She has invited him to explore different ways in which he might work with the authors. She notices that she is not enjoying the session. She is beginning to feel it is all rather helpless. It seems impossible that the authors will respond any differently.

Rowena realizes that she is now feeling helpless – and impotent to help Brian. As she becomes aware of this she notes that this is something she often feels with Brian but she does not recognize it as a pattern of her own. Perhaps she is experiencing this on Brian's behalf?

Rowena Brian, I'm wondering how you are feeling about sorting this out – whether it's possible or not?

Brian Well, actually I think it's pretty hopeless. I can't see how authors will ever stop feeling criticized when I make changes.

Rowena realizes she may be experiencing how powerless

Brian feels, and she uses this to guide herself.

Rowena I think I really do understand how helpless it
feels.

Brian meets her look more directly for a moment and
there is emotion in his eyes, perhaps as he realizes his
struggle is being seen. Rowena feels empathy for Brian as
he struggles to handle this problem.

   She also suddenly feels she can see things more clearly
and at that moment realizes that Brian is probably
projecting his fear of being criticized onto the authors too.

TRANSPARENCY AND SELF-DISCLOSURE

The coach/pupil relationship differs from ordinary social
relationships in that the coach is available primarily for the
benefit of the pupil. In this chapter I have presented some of
the processes that can arise in this relationship and how they
can be shaped by this asymmetry.

   You may recall telling someone about a problem you
have been having, only to experience them say something like
'Yes, I remember when . . .' and then they tell their own story
or one about someone they know. Sometimes it is good to
hear that others have similar experiences, but often the telling
of someone else's experiences can take attention away from
where it is most needed at this time. The would-be helper
may, for example, be diverting attention away because it is less
uncomfortable than staying with the immediate problems of
the person being helped. One characteristic of an effective
helping relationship is that helpers set to one side their own
needs to focus on the needs of those they are helping. This
often includes abstaining from talking about themselves or
their experience, to keep the focus on the person they are
helping.

   Many professional helpers, such as some counsellors and

Telling your story may be distracting.

psychotherapists, are trained to reveal virtually nothing personal of themselves. Others take the view that appropriate self-disclosure by the helper is an important part of establishing a relationship in which the person being helped is free to make relevant disclosures. Mutual sharing can contribute to a real meeting between the two persons. Sidney Jourard (1971) has shown that patients in the care of nurses who self-disclose fare better than those in the care of non-disclosing nurses. My experience is that self-disclosure can be enormously helpful when well judged, but diversionary and even destructive when used indiscriminately.

Judged well, sharing your experience can be very helpful.

Wise coaches will therefore note impulses to tell of their experience and check whether to do so really is in the pupil's interest. Simply being aware of this choice is a key first step in avoiding the trap of self-disclosing in an unhelpful way. I find the following structure helpful when considering disclosing of myself in a coaching situation:

1. Note my impulse to tell of my own experience.
2. Reflect on whether this is a need of my own or arises because I feel it may be helpful to the pupil.
3. If I decide to disclose:
   - say just a sentence or two;
   - check whether the pupil is engaging with what I am saying. If not, say no more. Otherwise continue, but *keep it brief*;
   - then return the focus to the pupil.

Let us look at an example:

Rowena continues to work with Brian. She is now aware that Brian feels helpless to improve his relationship with his authors because he imagines that he will be seen by them as critical, and he fears criticism himself.

Rowena suddenly feels compassion for Brian as she recalls her fear of criticism, and she decides to share this with him.

Rowena   I see how sensitive you are to possible criticism and I feel for you. I fear it too.

Brian   [Looks interested] Really?

Rowena   [Deciding to continue] Oh, yes. You know, I've been nervous about introducing this coaching approach, because I fear criticism from John about me being less in control.

There is a moment in which they seem to meet together in their shared experience, and then Rowena brings the focus back to Brian.

Rowena   So when you say you fear being criticized, I really understand ... but I also know that the fear is often worse than the reality. So I think it might be helpful for you to review here the different ways in which you might work with the authors, both critical and non-critical.

Brian   Yes, I think that would be helpful.

EXPLORING COACHING RELATIONSHIPS

Exercise 25 gives you the opportunity to look at your coaching relationships.

Exercise 25 – Exploring coaching relationships

Find some time (say 30 minutes) when you can be private and uninterrupted. You might prefer to do this away from the office. Have some paper to make notes.

1. Reflect upon the relationship you have with your coach or manager.
   - What are the issues that you do not discuss? Make a list. If this is short, take some more time to develop it further.
   - What do you imagine would happen if you talked completely openly about the things on your list?
   - How is your list and your choice not to discuss them

influenced by your past experience of (a) previous bosses; (b) school years; (c) childhood?

2. Now reflect upon your relationship with a coaching pupil.
   - What are the issues that you do not discuss? Make a list.
   - What do you imagine the pupil may not be discussing with you? Make a list. If this is short, take some more time.
   - Alongside each of the things you imagine your pupil may not be discussing, make a note of how you contribute to the pupil's choice not to discuss this issue.
3. If you were to share openly with your coach or manager and this pupil, what could you tell them from your experience in this exercise?

Note that I am not suggesting that you necessarily share all these thoughts with the other persons. This exercise will be most helpful if you are open and honest with yourself, and you are free to find aspects you would not wish to share.

It should be your choice as to which of your discoveries you choose to share with others. Your relationships with them will in any event develop, whether you speak of these discoveries or not.

ACTION LIST
1. Having studied this chapter and the example sessions, do Exercise 25.
2. Decide what you would like to develop in your relationships.
3. Consider what you can do to help bring this about.
4. Decide when you are going to act on this.

POSTSCRIPT

When Rowena was considering adopting the coaching approach she discussed her concerns with her boss John. They agreed to have a general review of her position after six months. In this final section of the book, let us drop in on that review.

John	So, how do you think it's going?
Rowena	Well, mostly rather well, although it's not all been easy.
John	What's gone well?
Rowena	I feel my team have really welcomed my adopting the coaching approach with them, and they've in turn taken to coaching their people. We've all enjoyed the time we've set aside to practise, and learned to be more open with each other when struggling to get the hang of something.
John	And what's been less easy?
Rowena	Making the time for the practice sessions, but we knew that was going to be difficult from the beginning. As we've started to see benefits it's been easier to make the time.

John   What aspects of the coaching process were difficult to take on?

Rowena   I think learning to hold back on solving other people's problems, and realizing the task is to support them in solving their own problems. I somewhat felt in the early stages that time spent away from solving the problems was unjustified, sort of not getting on with the real work. I've spent quite a bit of time with some of my people on quite personal issues – like their fears of criticism or not coping – which I once thought were not appropriate in the work context. But I've seen how these concerns were inhibiting them from contributing fully, and I feel now that it was a good investment. Things are beginning to go more smoothly.

John   I recall when you were starting on this you were rather nervous about it.

Rowena   Yes . . . I was unsure about how you would see it . . . What do you think?

John   You still seem nervous about that.

Rowena   Yes, I suppose I am. Perhaps I am afraid you will be critical of me.

John   That's rich! My concern was more that the other directors might question my supporting you in this. I also supposed that if they saw us making all these changes it would raise difficult questions as to why they were not doing the same.

Rowena   And has it?

John   Well, there have been some changes. I've had to put more time aside to work with you, but I notice I've had fewer members of your staff raising problems with me, and that seems a good trade-off. Your operation seems more self-contained.

I feel more comfortable about the financial

	balance of the last few issues, but I did get some flak from Western region because their returns were missing from the June consolidated report.
Rowena	Oh no! I knew I should have fitted their lateness in again.
John	I had a chat with Michael and pointed out that it's up to him to get his figures in on the agreed time scales. We cannot cover up indefinitely for the problems they are having.
Rowena	Oh, thanks.
John	Actually, Michael's been noticing the changes happening here, and he is rather impressed. What he'd really like is for someone to help him introduce coaching in his operation – how about it, Rowena?

APPENDICES

BRAINSTORMING

Brainstorming is a technique for developing ideas creatively and finding the radical idea that might not be reached by careful consideration. It can also help in identifying ideas that we might otherwise shy away from or self-censor. Brainstorming is best done in a group, so that the ideas of one person can trigger ideas in another. It is also possible for one person to do it alone.

Use a medium to record the ideas. A flip chart is ideal.

During the brainstorm, participants throw out their thoughts (ideas, possible solutions, etc.) and these are recorded without consideration or judgement. Any idea, no matter how 'way out' it might seem, is recorded. It is most creative if the ideas are not thought through at this stage so that a fast flow results.

It may be helpful to set a minimum time for this exercise (say ten minutes). The most interesting ideas may only emerge after the more obvious ones have been stated.

When the brainstorm has been completed, the ideas can be assessed. Some ideas can be eliminated and the list honed down to the useful ones.

Remember the key rules for brainstorming:

- Do not judge or censor ideas – give yourself freedom.
- Keep the ideas flowing.

- Never criticize someone's ideas as inappropriate, no matter how wild they may seem to you.

*V*ALUES AND BELIEFS FOR COACHING

In Exercise 6 you were invited to consider the values and beliefs that you feel would support the coaching process. In this appendix you will find the values and beliefs propounded by Kinlaw (1996) for superior coaching. You can use this to review your own list.

HUMAN COMPETENCY

Superior coaches believe that people:

- want to be competent and, given the necessary help, will strive to become more competent;
- must be given the opportunity to demonstrate their competency on a continual basis.

BASIS FOR SUPERIOR PERFORMANCE

Superior coaches share a commitment to superior performance, believing that:

- Managing and leading by control is not practicable and does not lead to a commitment to superior performance or the continuous improvement of performance.
- Superior performance results from the commitment of individuals and teams to perform at the best of their ability.
- Commitment is a function of at least the following conditions:
  - People understand what they are doing and why it is important.
  - People have the competencies to perform the jobs that are expected of them.
  - People feel appreciated for what they do.
  - People feel challenged by their jobs.
  - People have the chance to improve when they make mistakes.

VALUES OF COACHING

Superior coaches hold common values about the importance of coaching. They also share key values about how to coach, i.e. their understanding of coaching and the way they actually interact with people in their coaching conversations.

Superior coaches believe:

- that they must initiate coaching interactions and use every interaction with individuals and teams as a potential opportunity to coach – rather than to direct;
- in discipline, and view coaching as a set of competencies that can be learned and tested like any other set of skills required for managing and leading.

FEEDBACK AND CHECKLISTS

At various points in this book you are invited to give feedback to others, particularly as they practise their coaching skills. In this appendix I am offering some pointers and advice about feedback in this context.

Feedback is most beneficial if you can receive it without getting into discussion about it, or trying to justify your position. If there are surprises for you, I suggest you just reflect on what you are being offered, and notice any common patterns among different commentators. You do not have to accept what you are being offered, neither do you need to reject it there and then. You can mull it over and take what you want. If you still feel a strong need to say something a day later, then you can do so.

When giving feedback as an observer remember that your feedback is to the person who has been practising coaching skills, not to the pupil. Avoid getting into supplementary coaching as you would have done it, or adding to the work you have observed. Avoid using feedback to make 'digs' or comments to which the other person may need to respond. Table A3.1 is a useful 'pocket guide' to giving feedback.

TABLE A3.1: Good feedback in a nutshell

A useful mnemonic for the points on good feedback is **C O R B S:**

Clear	Be clear and concise. Avoid rambling on.
Owned	The feedback is your perception, not an absolute truth. 'I felt you were...' is acceptable as your view, whereas 'You were...' is not necessarily true and the recipient may feel a need to defend themselves.
Regular	In general feedback should be given a little and often. Avoid saving it up into a large package.
Balanced	Feedback should be balanced between positive and negative.
Specific	Be specific or concrete. Generalized feedback is hard to learn from. 'You were vague' is not as helpful as 'I felt you were vague about exactly what follow-up action was required.'

In Chapter 7 you were invited to practise your coaching in threes or one-to-one. This appendix contains tables of checklists to help you in giving this feedback.

TABLE A3.2: Feedback checklist for observers

1.	Quality of attention by the coach	What contributed? What detracted?
2.	Attention to the field	How was this done?
3.	Agreeing aims	Were they agreed? Were they clear or fuzzy?
4.	Listening	What indications of listening?
5.	Reflecting	Was reflecting used?
6.	Awareness	Was there a development of awareness? How was this achieved?
7.	Focusing	How was the session focused?
8.	Analysis	Was there analysis of the issues?
9.	Teaching	What teaching was used?
10.	Action	What actions were agreed?
11.	Assessment	Was there an assessment of the session?
12.	Overall shape	Did the session have a clear shape?
13.	Which interventions were most helpful?	
14.	Which interventions were least helpful or unhelpful?	

TABLE A3.3: Feedback checklist for pupils

1.	Quality of attention you received	What contributed?
		What detracted?
2.	Attention to the field	Did you have any concerns (relevant or irrelevant) which were not addressed?
3.	Agreeing aims	Did you become clear what the session was about?
4.	Listening	How well heard did you feel?
5.	Reflecting	How accurately did your coach understand you?
6.	Awareness	Did you discover new perspectives on the issue?
7.	Focusing	How was the session focused?
8.	Analysis	How were you led to analyse the issues?
9.	Teaching	What new skills did you learn?
10.	Action	Is it clear what actions you now need to take?
11.	Assessment	Did you have any feedback for your coach that you did not give?
12.	Overall shape	Did you feel comfortable with the shape of the session?
13.	Which interventions were most helpful?	
14.	Which interventions were least helpful or unhelpful?	

TABLE A3.4: Feedback checklist for coaches

1.	Quality of attention	Did you feel able to give your pupil 'quality attention'?
2.	Attention to the field	Was anything intruding on your thoughts that was not dealt with? Was your pupil distracted?
3.	Agreeing aims	What aims did you identify? Were they clear?
4.	Listening	Were you aware of listening for what the pupil was saying?
5.	Reflecting	Were you aware of reflecting? Did your pupil correct any inaccurate reflections?
6.	Awareness	What new awareness of the issues did your pupil develop? What new awareness did you gain?
7.	Focusing	How did you focus the session?
8.	Analysis	Was there analysis of the issues?
9.	Teaching	What teaching did you do?
10.	Action	What actions were agreed?
11.	Assessment	Did you get an assessment of your session, or are you still unclear how useful it was?
12.	Overall shape	Did the session have a clear shape?

13. Which interventions were most helpful?

14. Which interventions were least helpful or unhelpful?

REFERENCES

Egan, Gerard (1986) *The Skilled Helper*, Brook/Cole, California.

Hennessy, John (1983) *Torvill & Dean*, David & Charles, London.

Jourard, Sydney (1971) *The Transparent Self*, Van Nostrand Reinhold, New York.

Kinlaw, Dennis (1996) *Coaching: The ASTD Trainer's Source Book*, McGraw-Hill, New York.

McGregor, Douglas (1960) *The Human Side of Enterprise*, McGraw-Hill, New York.

Myers, M. Scott (1970) *Every Employee a Manager*, McGraw-Hill, New York.

INDEX